HALL OF FAME
of
Southern
RECIPES

White Chocolate and Lime Mousse Cake

HALL OF FAME

of

Southern

RECIPES

ALL-TIME FAVORITE RECIPES FROM SOUTHERN AMERICA

Gwen McKee and Barbara Moseley

QUAIL RIDGE PRESS

Preserving America's Food Heritage

Recipe Collection ©2012 Quail Ridge Press

All Rights Reserved

No part of this book may be reproduced or utilized in any form without written permission from the publisher.

ISBN–13: 978–1-934193-22-8
ISBN–10: 1-934193-22-4

On the cover: Strawberry Pecan Cake (page 138), Buttercup Biscuits (page 27), Mint Fruit Tea (page 10), Savannah Cheese Grits with Breakfast Shrimp (page 40)

Design by Cynthia Clark

Strawberry Pecan Cake on front cover plus photos on pages 138, 153, 171, 185, 191, and 201 by Greg Campbell

Printed in the United States of America

First edition, March 2012

Library of Congress Cataloging-in-Publication Data

McKee, Gwen.
　　Hall of fame of southern recipes : all-time favorite recipes from southern America / Gwen McKee & Barbara Moseley.—1st ed.
　　　p. cm.
　　Includes index.
　　ISBN 978-1-934193-22-8 (1-934193-22-4)
　1. Cooking, American—Southern style. 2. Cookbooks. I. Moseley, Barbara. II. Title.
　　TX715.2.S68M347 2012
　　641.5975—dc23　　　　　　　　　　　　2011043790

About the Photography:
The food photographs in this book were taken by Quail Ridge Press staff member Emily Mills Burkett (except those mentioned above by Greg Campbell Photography). All food in the photographs was purchased at ordinary grocery stores and prepared exactly to recipe directions. No artificial food-styling techniques were used to enhance the food's appearance. Only water was sometimes spritzed on the food to keep it looking fresh during the photo shoot.

QUAIL RIDGE PRESS
P. O. Box 123 • Brandon, MS 39043
info@quailridge.com • www.quailridge.com
www.facebook.com/cookbookladies

Contents

Slow-Roasted Onion Soup

Preface

Barbara and I started our BEST OF THE BEST STATE COOKBOOK SERIES in 1982. Being natives of Louisiana and Mississippi, we naturally began this venture in the South. In the early years, we did not have the benefit of the Internet, a GPS, or even a cell phone when we loaded our van and traveled throughout the eleven-state southern region—Arkansas to Virginia. Our goal was to find choice cookbooks within each state that contained those family recipe gems. These discoveries might come from

recognized Junior League cookbooks in big cities, but also from modest cookbooks published in small communities.

Along the way on our mission to discover the best recipes from the best cookbooks, we met many friendly people who were eager to help

us. We learned firsthand what people in their state liked to cook and eat. They also directed us to restaurants and cafés where the locals liked to dine. These occasions often led to discussions of food and recipes. Our face-to-face dealings with local people in communities throughout each state were not only valuable to our compiling the BEST OF THE BEST STATE COOKBOOKS, but were the most enjoyable and memorable part of our research.

We have now completed the entire fifty states in this Series, and a considerable number of totally new editions, of mostly the southern states. From this database of over 8,000 southern recipes, and from our own personal experience of southern cooking, we have selected 212 HALL OF FAME recipes that capture the essence and flavor of this region.

We have included classic southern dishes, and have selected the recipes that we feel deliver the "Best" results. Among the array of classics included are Aunt Martha's Buttermilk Cornbread, Savannah Cheese Grits, Sauced Sweet Potatoes, Southern Fried Catfish, Toasted Butter Pecan Cake, Georgia Blackberry Cobbler . . . and wait till you taste the Chocolate Cream Supreme! Yum, yum . . . and more yum.

Only the very best recipes make it into our acclaimed RECIPE HALL OF FAME. We like to say, "You don't have to visit the RECIPE HALL OF FAME . . . you can serve and enjoy it in your own home." So here it is! The Best of the BEST OF THE BEST from the South!

We are proud to present the *Hall of Fame of Southern Recipes*, which will enable everyone to know—and taste—the sheer joy of southern cooking.

Gwen McKee

Beverages & Appetizers

Mint Fruit Tea

Elegantly refreshing.

2 long stems of mint
Grated rind of ½ lemon
Grated rind of ½ orange
4 tea bags, or 2 tablespoons
    loose tea
2 cups boiling water
⅓ cup sugar

3¾ cups cold water
Juice of ½ orange
Juice of ½ lemon
Slices of lemon and orange for
    garnish
Sprigs of mint for garnish

Combine stems of mint, grated rinds, and tea in a heat-proof pitcher or teapot. Pour boiling water over all. Steep 10 minutes. Put remaining ingredients in a large pitcher or jar. Strain steeped tea mixture into pitcher and blend. Cool, and pour into tall glasses of ice. Garnish with thin slices of orange or lemon and sprigs of mint. Serves 6–8.

The Grace of Patti's (Kentucky)

Champagne Punch

3 cups sugar
2 cups lemon juice (not frozen)
1 (20-ounce) can pineapple
  chunks and juice
1 quart chilled Sauterne wine

1½ quarts chilled sparkling
  water
1 (16-ounce) bag whole frozen
  strawberries
2 bottles chilled champagne

Mix first 3 ingredients well, and chill. Just before serving, add remaining ingredients. Float an ice ring in serving bowl to keep chilled. Serves 30.

A Heritage of Good Tastes (Arkansas)

Editor's Extra: An ice ring melts more slowly than ice cubes. If you don't have a ring (to fill with water and freeze), use a shallow bowl. Pretty to add a few mint leaves, or tint with a few drops of food coloring before freezing.

Grandmother's Eggnog

6 eggs
4 tablespoons sugar
5 tablespoons bourbon
1 tablespoon rum

2 cups whipping cream
½ teaspoon salt
Nutmeg to taste
1 teaspoon vanilla

Separate eggs, keeping whites cold until used. Beat yolks until light. Add sugar, a little at a time, beating well as you add it. Then add bourbon and rum a teaspoon at a time. (It is important to add bourbon slowly so that the egg yolks get well cooked and won't have a raw taste.) Whip the cream; add to mixture, then add well-beaten whites, a grating or two of nutmeg (according to taste), and vanilla. Allow to ripen for at least 12 hours, which improves the taste. Refrigerate until ready to use, and mix well before serving.

Korner's Folly Cookbook (Mississippi)

Editor's Extra : It was once thought bourbon "cooked" eggs in the way vinegar cooks raw fish in seviche. In consuming raw and lightly cooked eggs, due to the slight risk of salmonella or other food-borne illness, we use only fresh, properly refrigerated, clean grade A or AA eggs with intact shells, and avoid contact between the yolks or whites and the shell.

Baked Vidalia Onion Dip

This is a great appetizer, and delicious with steaks or pork chops.

1 tablespoon milk	1–2 Vidalia onions, chopped
1 (8-ounce) package cream cheese, softened	small
3 ounces grated Parmesan cheese	

Mix milk, cream cheese, and Parmesan together with a mixer. Stir in onions. Place in a 1½-quart baking dish that has been sprayed with cooking spray. Bake at 350° for 30–40 minutes or until onions are bubbly and tender. Serve with crackers. Serves 8 or more.

Aliant Cooks for Education (Alabama)

Reuben Dip

1 (3-ounce) package cream
   cheese, softened
½ cup shredded Swiss cheese
4 ounces sliced corn beef,
   finely diced
¼ cup sour cream
¼ cup drained sauerkraut,
   chopped
2–3 tablespoons milk

Heat all ingredients in small saucepan over low heat. Thin with milk, if necessary. Serve with rye sticks. Serves 6 or more.

Florida Flavors (Florida)

Hot Cheesy Black-Eyed Pea Dip

A "must" for New Year's parties. Yum!

1 medium onion, chopped
2 tablespoons butter
½ cup sour cream
½ cup mayonnaise
1 (16-ounce) can black-eyed
   peas, drained, rinsed
1 envelope buttermilk ranch
   salad dressing mix
1 (14-ounce) can artichoke
   hearts, drained, chopped
1 cup shredded mozzarella
   cheese
2 tablespoons grated Parmesan
   cheese

Sauté onion in butter in skillet. In a medium bowl, combine onion with remaining ingredients, and mix well. Spoon into a baking dish. Bake at 350° for 20 minutes. Serve with crackers or tortilla chips. Yields 10–12 servings.

Beyond Cotton Country (Alabama)

Editor's Extra: If you have several dips for a party, tape a small "flag" with the recipe title onto a long toothpick, so your guests know what they are enjoying.

Fireside Dip

A delicious chili dip . . . great for a chilly night!

2 pounds hot bulk sausage
1 onion, chopped
3 garlic cloves, crushed
2 teaspoons chili powder
½ teaspoon ground cumin
3 (15-ounce) cans chili without
 beans
1 (1-pound) processed cheese
 spread loaf, cut into cubes

8 ounces Monterey Jack cheese,
 cut into cubes
2–3 jalapeño peppers, seeded
 and chopped
2 (10-ounce) cans diced tomatoes
 and green chiles, drained

Cook sausage, onion, and garlic in large saucepan over medium heat, stirring often, until sausage crumbles and is no longer pink; drain well. Add chili powder, cumin, chili, cheeses, jalapeño peppers, and tomatoes and green chiles to mixture, stirring well. Cook over medium heat, stirring constantly, until cheese is melted.

Serve dip hot in a chafing dish with home-fried tortilla chips. Serves 25–30.

Absolutely à la Carte (Mississippi)

Hot Cheese Puffs

1 loaf firm white unsliced bread
3 ounces cream cheese
¼ pound sharp Cheddar cheese,
   grated

½ cup butter
2 egg whites, stiffly beaten

Trim bread and cut in 1-inch cubes. In the top of a double boiler, melt cheeses and butter, cool, and fold in stiffly beaten egg whites. With a fork, pick up bread cubes and dip them, one at a time, into the cheese mixture. Ease off fork with knife onto cookie sheet. Refrigerate overnight, or freeze. Bake at 400° until fluffy and brown. If frozen, no need to thaw before baking. May be doubled. Yields about 100 small puffs.

The Belle Grove Plantation Cookbook (Virginia)

Shrimp Puffs

1 pound boiled shrimp, peeled
   and finely chopped
1 small onion, finely chopped
1 clove garlic, finely chopped
Black pepper to taste

1 cup all-purpose flour
2 teaspoons baking powder
1 teaspoon salt
Dash of red pepper
Milk

Mix together all ingredients, except milk. Add milk a little at a time until mixture forms a stiff dough. Drop into hot grease about 3 inches deep, a teaspoon at a time. Fry fast until golden brown. Drain on paper towels. Yields 40–50.

Recipes and Reminiscences of New Orleans II (Louisiana)

Hot Seafood Mornay

This is excellent for do-ahead. Guests, both at home and at catered affairs, have raved over this dip. Enjoy!

4 tablespoons butter
2 tablespoons olive oil
½ cup chopped green onions
½ cup chopped onion
½ cup chopped bell pepper
½ cup chopped celery
1 (14-ounce) can mushroom
  stems and pieces, drained
3 teaspoons jarred minced garlic
3 (8-ounce) packages cream
  cheese, softened
¼ cup mayonnaise

3 tablespoons Dijon mustard
2 tablespoons dried parsley
½ cup dry sherry
½ cup grated Parmesan cheese
½ cup shredded mozzarella
  cheese
1 (1-pound) package crawfish
  tails, thawed
1 pound shrimp, boiled, deveined,
  and coarsely chopped
1 pound lump crabmeat

Melt butter in saucepan; add olive oil, and sauté next 6 ingredients until tender. Blend in cream cheese, mayonnaise, and mustard until smooth. Add parsley, sherry, Parmesan, and mozzarella cheese, and mix well. Gradually mix in crawfish tails, shrimp, and lump crabmeat. If mixture is too thin, add flour to thicken.

Transfer mixture to chafing dish casserole, and sprinkle top with additional Parmesan cheese, dried parsley, and paprika. Bake at 350° for 30 minutes until bubbly and golden brown on top. Serve with Melba rounds, toast points, or crackers. Serves 25 or more.

Lagniappe: Secrets We're Ready to Share (Mississippi)

Fried Pickles

1 cup all-purpose flour
¼ teaspoon salt
Black pepper to taste
1 egg

¼ cup milk
Vegetable oil
1½ cups sliced dill pickles, drained
Ranch dressing for dipping

Mix flour, salt, and pepper in a bowl. Lightly whip egg and milk in a separate bowl. Heat oil (about 2 inches) to 375°. Dip pickle slices first into flour mixture, then egg mixture, and finally back into flour. Carefully place pickles into hot oil. Do not overcrowd. Fry until golden brown, 4–8 minutes, turning once. Drain on paper towels. Serve warm with ranch dressing. Serves 6 or more.

Best Kept Secrets (South Carolina)

Creole Marinated Crab Claws

Big on healthy, bigger on tasty.

⅓ cup extra virgin olive oil
½ cup defatted chicken broth, less salt
½ cup wine vinegar
⅓ cup lemon juice
2 green onions, chopped
2 tablespoons minced garlic
1 tablespoon black pepper
1 teaspoon celery seed or flakes
¼ cup parsley flakes
1 teaspoon light Creole seasoning
1 pound crab claws, rinsed and drained
Cherry tomatoes and black olives for garnish

Mix marinade (all ingredients except crab claws and garnishes), and pour over crab claws in shallow dish. Refrigerate for at least 4 hours. Drain well, and serve on a platter lined with lettuce leaves. Garnish with cherry tomatoes and black olives. Yields 6 servings.

Per Serving: Cal 101; Fat 6.6g; %Fat Cal 57; Sat Fat 0.9g; Chol 24mg; Sod 136mg.

River Road Recipes III (Louisiana)

Kentucky Country Ham Balls

2 pounds Kentucky country ham, ground
1 pound Parnell's Old Folks Country Sausage
2 cups dry bread crumbs
2 eggs
1½–2 cups milk
2 cups packed brown sugar
1 cup water
1 cup white vinegar
1 tablespoon prepared mustard

Combine ham, sausage, bread crumbs, and eggs in a large bowl, and mix well. Add milk gradually (enough to moisten), and mix well. Shape into small balls, and place in a single layer in a baking dish.

Combine brown sugar, water, vinegar, and mustard in saucepan, and mix well. Bring to a boil, then pour over ham balls. Bake at 350° for 45 minutes, basting after 25 minutes. Yields 8 dozen.

Splendor in the Bluegrass (Kentucky)

Hot and Spicy Cocktail Meatballs

Make these party-pleaser meatballs ahead; freeze for later.

MEATBALLS:

¾ pound ground beef
1½ teaspoons minced onion
3 drops Tabasco
¾ teaspoon salt

¾ cup fine dry bread crumbs
½ teaspoon prepared horseradish
2 eggs, beaten
½ teaspoon pepper

Mix all ingredients for Meatballs, and shape into ¾-inch balls. Melt 1 tablespoon butter in electric skillet set at 340°. Add Meatballs, and brown. Stir frequently for even browning and to keep balls round. When browned and done, pour off any fat, then add Sauce.

SAUCE:

¾ cup ketchup
¼ cup cider vinegar
1 tablespoon minced onion
¼ teaspoon pepper

½ cup water
2 tablespoons brown sugar
2 teaspoons dry mustard
3 drops Tabasco

Combine Sauce ingredients. Add to browned Meatballs, cover, and continue to cook about 10 minutes, stirring occasionally. Can be made the day ahead or frozen.

To serve, put in chafing dish and keep hot. Yields about 4½ dozen Meatballs.

The Pick of the Crop (Mississippi)

Baby Hot Browns

1 chicken bouillon cube	6 ounces turkey deli meat
¼ cup hot water	1 onion, sliced thin
¾ cup half-and-half	18 slices party rye or small
3 tablespoons unsalted butter	French bread
2 tablespoons all-purpose flour	5 strips bacon, cooked, crumbled
1 cup grated Swiss cheese	Parsley

Dissolve bouillon cube in hot water; add half-and-half. In a saucepan, melt butter and add flour. Whisk and cook until mixture is frothy and raw flour taste is gone. While stirring, add bouillon mixture. Stir constantly with a whisk until sauce thickens and begins to bubble. Remove from heat. Add Swiss cheese, and stir until smooth. (If sauce needs to be thinned, heat with a little added water.)

Assemble hot browns by placing turkey and onion on each bread slice. Top with sauce and crumbled bacon. Garnish with parsley. Yields 18.

The Kentucky Derby Museum Cook Book (Kentucky)

Editor's Extra: Don't hesitate to put this on any size or type of brown bread. Great for lunch, too.

Luscious Pimento Cheese

This southern staple is traditionally used for sandwiches, but is equally great on crackers or apple slices. Yum!

1½ pounds extra sharp white Cheddar cheese, grated
1 (10-ounce) jar stuffed green olives, drained, chopped
1 (12-ounce) jar roasted red peppers, drained, chopped
½ cup freshly grated Parmesan cheese
½ cup mayonnaise
2 tablespoons chopped parsley
½ teaspoon freshly ground black pepper
¼ teaspoon cayenne pepper
1 tablespoon minced onion
½ cup sliced almonds, toasted

Combine all ingredients. Refrigerate several hours before serving. Serves 12 or more.

Faithfully Charleston (South Carolina)

Cream Cheese with Jezebel Sauce

Great replacement for pepper jelly. Also a wonderful gift idea. May also be served with roast beef or pork.

1 (18-ounce) jar pineapple
   preserves
1 (18-ounce) jar apple jelly
1 (5-ounce) jar prepared
   horseradish

1 (1-ounce) can dry mustard
1 tablespoon cracked peppercorns
1 package cream cheese (any size),
   softened

In a bowl, combine preserves, jelly, horseradish, mustard, and peppercorns, mixing well. Pour into airtight containers. Cover, and store in refrigerator. Serve over cream cheese as a spread accompanied with crackers. Yields approximately 4 cups of sauce.

Virginia Seasons (Virginia)

Pepper Jelly

1 cup ground bell pepper
2 tablespoons ground hot
   peppers
1½ cups cider vinegar

6½ cups sugar
Green food coloring
1 (6-ounce) bottle liquid fruit
   pectin

Mix everything except fruit pectin in saucepan, and bring to a boil. Let boil for 5 minutes, remove from heat, and add fruit pectin, stirring until mixture starts to jell. Pour into sterile jelly jars, and seal. (This is good spooned over a brick of cream cheese and served with ginger snaps.) Yields 3–6 jars, depending on size.

The Farmer's Daughters (Arkansas)

Editor's Extra: Offer this with pork or turkey—delicious!

Boursin Cheese—Home Style

8 ounces whipped butter,
   softened
16 ounces cream cheese,
   softened
2 cloves garlic, minced
½ teaspoon oregano

¼ teaspoon basil
¼ teaspoon dill weed
¼ teaspoon marjoram
¼ teaspoon black pepper
¼ teaspoon thyme

Place butter and cream cheese in large bowl of an electric mixer or food processor. Beat at high speed till smooth and fluffy, stopping motor often to scrape down sides of bowl with a rubber spatula. Add remaining ingredients, and continue to beat until well combined. Pack into containers, and allow to mellow for at least 12 hours in refrigerator before serving. Serve cold with crackers.

Note: Okay to prepare in advance: if wrapped airtight, this will keep for 2 weeks to a month. Do not freeze.

Feast and Fellowship (Georgia)

Editor's Extra: Pretty to fluff before serving.

Bread & Breakfast

Quick Rolls

1 cup milk
3 tablespoons shortening
1 package yeast

2 cups all-purpose flour
3 teaspoons sugar
1 teaspoon salt

Heat milk and shortening to lukewarm. Add yeast to the mixture. Add flour, sugar, and salt; beat well. Place on floured dough board. Roll and cut. Place rolls on lightly greased baking pan. Let rise for 1 hour, and bake in 400° oven till lightly browned (15–20 minutes). Yields 12–18 rolls.

A Heritage of Good Tastes (Arkansas)

Never-Fail Pan Rolls

¾ cup sugar
¾ cup shortening
1 cup boiling water
2 packages dry yeast
1 cup warm water

2 eggs, slightly beaten
6–7 cups all-purpose flour, divided
1 teaspoon salt
1 teaspoon baking powder
½ teaspoon baking soda

In large mixing bowl, cream sugar and shortening till light and fluffy. Add boiling water. Mix thoroughly, and let cool. In small mixing bowl, dissolve yeast in warm water, and set aside.

Add eggs to cooled shortening mixture, and mix well. Stir in yeast mixture. Combine 5 cups flour with salt, baking powder, and baking soda. Add to yeast mixture, and mix well. Turn out dough onto well-floured surface. Knead in enough remaining flour till dough is no longer sticky. Roll into 1½-inch balls. Place balls, nearly touching, in greased 9-inch round cake pans. Cover, and let rolls rise in warm place till doubled. Bake at 400° for 20 minutes. Yields 3 dozen.

Note: This dough will keep in refrigerator for a week.

Coastal Carolina Cooking (North Carolina)

Buttercup Biscuits

This recipe won first prize in our "Easter Brunch Contest."

2 sticks butter, softened   **2 cups presifted self-rising flour**
1 (8-ounce) container sour cream

Blend butter and sour cream until creamy. Add flour; mix. Drop dough by teaspoonfuls into buttercup-size mini muffin pans. Bake 30–35 minutes at 350°, or until golden brown. Yields 4 dozen.

Kum' Ona' Granny's Table (Alabama)

Garlic-Cheese Biscuits

BISCUITS:
2 (7-ounce) packages buttermilk
   biscuit mix
⅔ cup buttermilk
½ cup shredded sharp Cheddar
   cheese

Mix ingredients, and drop dough by teaspoonfuls onto greased cookie sheet. Bake at 450° for 8–10 minutes. Yields about 20.

TOPPING:
½ cup butter, melted
1 teaspoon minced garlic
1 teaspoon parsley flakes

Mix ingredients. As soon as Biscuits come out of oven, brush with Topping.

A Taste of Heaven (Kentucky)

Aunt Martha's Buttermilk Cornbread

3 tablespoons all-purpose flour
1¼ cups cornmeal
1 teaspoon salt
¾ teaspoon baking powder
1 cup buttermilk
2 small eggs, beaten
2 tablespoons shortening
½ teaspoon baking soda

Mix flour, cornmeal, salt, and baking powder. Add buttermilk to beaten eggs. Melt shortening. Cut both mixtures into dry ingredients. Add baking soda that has been dissolved in a little water (2 tablespoons). Pour into hot greased skillet or pan, and bake at 425° until done (about 25 minutes). Yields 6 servings.

Smokehouse Ham, Spoon Bread, & Scuppernong Wine (Tennessee)

Broccoli Cornbread

This is so good, moist, and delicious!

1 (8-ounce) box Jiffy cornbread mix
4 eggs, beaten
1 stick butter, melted
1 onion, chopped fine
2 cups (8 ounces) grated Cheddar cheese
1 (10-ounce) box frozen broccoli, thawed

Combine all ingredients, and mix well. Pour mixture into a 9x13-inch pan or 9x9-inch square baking dish that has been sprayed with non-stick cooking spray. Bake at 350° for about 30 minutes. Serves 6 or more.

Endless Praise Dishes (Alabama)

Editor's Extra: If the 10-ounce boxes of frozen vegetables are not available, you can use about ⅔ of a 16-ounce bag.

Jalapeño Hush Puppies
"The World's Best"

2 cups cornmeal
1 cup all-purpose flour
2 eggs, beaten
3 teaspoons baking powder
1½ teaspoons salt
1 (8-ounce) can cream-style corn

3 jalapeño peppers, chopped
¼ bell pepper, chopped
1 small onion, minced
Pinch of baking soda
Buttermilk

Mix all ingredients. Use enough buttermilk to make this the consistency of cornbread batter. Test batter by scooping up a portion on a spoon and, with your thumb, push portion into medium hot grease. The object of this recipe is to have light, fluffy hush puppies. If heavy and do not rise enough, use more baking powder. If hush puppies are greasy and break apart, add more flour. If you want more tang, add some jalapeño pepper juice. Serves 6 or more.

The Cotton Country Collection (Louisiana)

Eva's Hush Puppies

2 cups self-rising cornmeal
1 cup self-rising flour
2 small onions, diced
1 small bell pepper, diced
3 eggs

1 (15¼-ounce) can whole-kernel
  yellow corn, undrained
1 tablespoon sugar
2½ tablespoons vegetable oil
Oil for frying

Mix cornmeal, flour, onions, and bell pepper in a large mixing bowl, then add eggs, corn, sugar, and oil. The batter should be fairly stiff, not soupy like cornbread. Drop by tablespoonfuls into hot, deep oil. As it cooks and browns on one side, it will flip over and brown on the other side. Check with a fork on the first 2 or 3 to check the amount of time needed for each batch.

Feeding the Flock (Florida)

Cajun Crawfish Cornbread

2 cups cornmeal
1 teaspoon salt
1 teaspoon baking powder
6 eggs
2 medium onions, chopped

½ cup chopped jalapeño peppers
1 pound shredded Cheddar cheese
⅔ cup vegetable oil
2 (14¾-ounce) cans cream corn
2 pounds crawfish tails

In bowl, combine cornmeal, salt, and baking powder. In medium bowl, beat eggs, chopped onions, and jalapeño peppers. Grate cheese and add beaten eggs, onions, peppers, cheese, oil, corn, and crawfish tails. Combine this mixture with cornmeal mixture; mix well. Pour into greased 9x13-inch baking dish. Bake at 375° for 55 minutes or until golden brown. Serves 10 or more.

Family Favorites (Louisiana)

Editor's Extra: Vegetable can sizes used to be 16 ounces, but have gotten smaller. Most recipes can accommodate the fluctuating sizes, from 14 to 16 ounces.

Sedberry Inn Pineapple Muffins

Everyone will want the recipe.

¾ cup butter, softened
1½ cups sugar
3 eggs, beaten
3 cups all-purpose flour

3 teaspoons baking powder
1 (20-ounce) can crushed pineapple
2 tablespoons orange extract

Cream butter and sugar; do not overbeat. Add beaten eggs and beat lightly. Add dry ingredients, then pineapple and orange extract, mixing only till blended. Bake in greased muffin tins at 350° for about 20 minutes (or 12 minutes for mini muffins). Do not allow muffins to brown on top. Ice while muffins are still warm. Yields 3 dozen regular or 6 dozen mini muffins.

ICING:
2 tablespoons milk
2 tablespoons butter

2 cups powdered sugar
2 tablespoons orange extract

In saucepan, heat milk and butter, but do not boil. Add powdered sugar and orange extract; mix well.

Out of the World (Tennessee)

Sunshine Muffins

Laden with fruit and nuts, these muffins bring a touch of tropical sunshine to any brunch or breakfast, and really don't need any additional spread.

½ cup milk
¼ cup vegetable oil
2 eggs
½ cup raisins
1½ cups rolled oats
2 cups baking mix
½ cup sugar

½ cup packed brown sugar
1 teaspoon cinnamon
½ cup shredded carrot
1 cup shredded apple
1 (20-ounce) can crushed
  pineapple, drained
¼ cup chopped walnuts

Combine milk, oil, and eggs in a medium bowl, and beat lightly. Stir in raisins and oats. Let stand for several minutes. Add baking mix, sugar, brown sugar, cinnamon, carrot, apple, pineapple, and walnuts, and mix just until moistened. Spoon into greased muffin cups, filling ½ full. Bake at 400° for 20 minutes or until golden brown. Serves 12.

Tropical Settings (Florida)

Carrot-Poppy Seed Muffins

½ cup all-purpose flour
½ cup whole-wheat flour
¼ cup brown sugar
1½ teaspoons baking powder
¼ teaspoon salt
1 egg, beaten

½ cup milk
2 tablespoons butter or
  margarine, melted
⅓ cup shredded carrots
3 tablespoons poppy seeds

Combine flours, sugar, baking powder, and salt; stir to mix well. In a separate bowl, combine the egg, milk, and melted margarine; add to dry ingredients. Stir until moist and lumpy batter forms. Stir in carrots and poppy seeds. Spoon batter into greased muffin tins. Bake at 375° for 20–25 minutes or until a toothpick inserted into center comes out clean. Yields 6 muffins (or 12 mini muffins baked 15 minutes).

Delightfully Southern (Georgia)

Banana Brunch Bread

Nutty and sweet! A great gift to make and take.

TOPPING:
½ cup chopped nuts   ½ teaspoon cinnamon
½ cup sugar

Combine all ingredients; set aside. (May be doubled, if desired.)

½ cup butter, softened   ½ cup sour cream
1 cup sugar   2 cups sifted all-purpose flour
2 eggs   1 teaspoon baking powder
1 cup mashed bananas   ¼ teaspoon salt
½ teaspoon vanilla   1 teaspoon baking soda

Preheat oven to 350°. Heavily grease 3 loaf pans. Cream butter and sugar until light. Beat in eggs, one at a time. Mix in bananas, vanilla, and sour cream. Sift together flour, baking powder, salt, and baking soda. Fold into creamed mixture, stirring only enough to moisten.

Sprinkle half of Topping on bottoms of prepared loaf pans. Spoon in batter, and sprinkle with remaining Topping. Bake at 350° for 45 minutes. Bread may be frozen after baking. Yields 3 loaves.

The Crowning Recipes of Kentucky (Kentucky)

Orange Pecan Bread

¼ cup butter or margarine,
  softened
¾ cup sugar
2 eggs, beaten
2 teaspoons grated orange rind
2 cups all-purpose flour

2½ teaspoons baking powder
1 teaspoon salt
¾ cup plus 2½ teaspoons orange
  juice, divided
½ cup chopped pecans
½ cup powdered sugar, sifted

Cream butter. Gradually add ¾ cup sugar, beating well. Add beaten eggs and grated orange rind. Mix well. Combine flour, baking powder, and salt. Add to creamed mixture alternately with ¾ cup orange juice, beginning and ending with flour mixture. Mix well after each addition. Stir in pecans. Pour batter into a greased 9x5x3-inch loaf pan. Bake at 350° for 50–55 minutes, or until a wooden pick inserted in center comes out clean. Cool loaf in pan for 10 minutes. Remove from pan and cool completely.

Combine remaining 2½ teaspoons orange juice and ½ cup powdered sugar. Drizzle over loaf. Wrap and store overnight before serving. Can be frozen. Serves 6–8.

The Great Cookbook (Alabama)

Caramel French Toast

Impress your overnight guests with this fabulous dish!

1½ cups firmly packed brown
   sugar
¾ cup butter or margarine
6 tablespoons light corn syrup
10 (1¼-inch) French bread
   slices
4 eggs, beaten

2½ cups milk
1 tablespoon vanilla
¼ teaspoon salt
3 tablespoons sugar
1½ teaspoons ground cinnamon
¼ cup butter or margarine, melted

In a medium saucepan, combine brown sugar, ¾ cup butter, and corn syrup. Cook over medium heat, stirring constantly for 5 minutes or until bubbly. Pour syrup evenly into a lightly greased 9x13-inch baking dish. Place bread slices over syrup. Combine eggs, milk, vanilla, and salt. Stir well, and pour over bread. Cover, and refrigerate at least 8 hours.

Preheat oven to 350°. Combine sugar and cinnamon. Sprinkle evenly over soaked bread. Drizzle ¼ cup melted butter over top. Bake, uncovered, 45–50 minutes, or until golden and bubbly. Serves 10.

Note: Caramel French Toast is also a fabulous dessert! Just add 1 cup chopped pecans to syrup mixture. To serve, top each serving with whipped cream and a fanned strawberry.

Prime Meridian (Mississippi)

Editor's Extra: We like to dust with powdered sugar and serve with fresh blueberries. Or blueberry syrup! Yum!

Creamed Bacon, Eggs and Cheese

Don't expect these to last long.

4 tablespoons butter
3 tablespoons all-purpose flour
1¼ cups half-and-half
¼ pound American cheese, grated
4 hard-cooked eggs, cut into cubes

2 teaspoons dehydrated parsley flakes
Salt and pepper to taste
Dry toast or patty shells
Paprika
8 slices bacon, cooked, drained, and crumbled

Melt butter in saucepan over low heat; add flour, stirring until blended. Turn heat to medium; add half-and-half all at once; stir constantly until smooth and thick. Add cheese and stir until melted. Combine eggs and parsley flakes with mixture, adding salt and pepper. Serve on toast or in patty shells topped with paprika and crumbled bacon. Serves 4.

Accent One (Mississippi)

Editor's Extra: We used mini phyllo shells for an impressive easy-to-eat brunch treat.

Virginia Ham and Broccoli O'Brien

Hearty and delicious for brunch or supper.

10–12 slices white bread,
  buttered
2 cups diced baked Virginia ham
1 (10-ounce) package frozen
  chopped broccoli, cooked
1 (24-ounce) package frozen
  hash brown potatoes O'Brien,
  thawed

½ cup chopped onion
3 cups shredded sharp Cheddar
  cheese
6 eggs, slightly beaten
2–2½ cups half-and-half
¼ teaspoon Dijon mustard
Salt and pepper to taste

In an 8x12-inch baking dish, layer in order: bread, ham, broccoli, potatoes, and onion. Top with cheese. In a medium mixing bowl, combine eggs, half-and-half, mustard, salt, and pepper; mix well. Pour over top of cheese. Cover, and refrigerate 8 hours or overnight.

Remove from refrigerator; let stand 30 minutes, then bake, uncovered, at 325° for 1 hour. Serves 6–8.

Virginia Cook Book (Virginia)

Garlic Grits

Light and fluffy, and simply great!

1 cup grits, cooked
1 stick butter
¾ pound grated American
  cheese

½–1 clove garlic, minced
1½ tablespoons Worcestershire
Tabasco to taste
2 egg whites

To hot grits add all remaining ingredients except egg whites. Cool. When cool, add stiffly beaten egg whites, and bake at 400° in lightly greased casserole for 20 minutes. Serves 6.

Recipe Jubilee! (Alabama)

Savannah Cheese Grits with Breakfast Shrimp

CHEESE GRITS:

2 cups milk
1 cup water
¾ teaspoon salt
1 cup quick-cooking grits
¼ teaspoon garlic powder
Dash of hot pepper sauce

1½ cups grated sharp or
  smoked Cheddar cheese
2 eggs, beaten
½ cup butter
Paprika for garnish

Combine milk, water, and salt in a 2-quart casserole dish. Microwave on HIGH 8–10 minutes or until boiling. Stir in grits. Microwave 2–3 minutes or until soft. Stir in garlic powder, pepper sauce, cheese, eggs, and butter. Mix well. Microwave on HIGH 4–5 minutes or until thickened. Sprinkle with paprika. Serves 8.

BREAKFAST SHRIMP:

3 tablespoons butter
1 medium onion, chopped
¼ green bell pepper, chopped
2 tablespoons all-purpose flour
1 pound raw shrimp, peeled
  and deveined
Water to cover

1 teaspoon salt (or less)
Dash of hot pepper sauce
1 teaspoon Worcestershire
4–5 tablespoons ketchup
2 tablespoons chopped fresh
  parsley
½ cup whipping cream

Melt butter in a medium skillet over medium heat. Add onion and bell pepper, and cook until tender. Stir in flour; cook and stir until bubbly. Cook 1 minute. Increase heat and add shrimp. Cook and stir 2 minutes, or until shrimp are pink. Add enough water to cover shrimp. Cook and stir until mixture thickens slightly. Add salt, pepper sauce, Worcestershire, ketchup, and parsley; stir. Simmer about 5 minutes. Adjust seasonings as needed. Stir in cream. Heat thoroughly, but do not bring to a boil. Serve immediately over plain or Cheese Grits. Serves 4. (You may double ingredients for shrimp.)

Variation: You may add sliced andouille or Lumber Jack sausage.

First Come, First Served...In Savannah (Georgia)

Sausage-Cheese-Grits Casserole

4 cups water
1 cup grits
3 cups shredded sharp Cheddar
   cheese, divided
2 tablespoons butter or
   margarine

2 teaspoons Worcestershire
¼ cup milk
1½ teaspoons garlic salt
1 egg, beaten
1 pound bulk sausage, cooked,
   drained

Bring water to a boil in large saucepan; stir in grits. Cover, and reduce heat. Cook, stirring occasionally, until done. Remove from heat; add 2 cups Cheddar cheese, butter, Worcestershire, milk, and garlic salt, stirring until cheese melts. Stir small amount of grits into beaten egg; add to remaining grits mixture, stirring constantly. Spoon half of grits into lightly greased baking dish; top with sausage. Spoon remaining grits over sausage. Cover, and chill at least 8 hours.

Let stand at room temperature for 30 minutes. Bake uncovered at 350° for 40 minutes. Sprinkle with remaining 1 cup Cheddar cheese, and bake an additional 5 minutes. Yields 8 servings.

Recipe from River Inn B&B, Anderson
Palmetto Hospitality Inn Style (South Carolina)

Soups, Stews & Chilis

Sweet Potato Soup

A fabulous soup with a sandwich, especially ham. But hearty enough to be a stand-alone supper.

2 tablespoons butter
2 tablespoons finely grated
   fresh ginger*
3 stalks celery, finely chopped
1 large onion, finely chopped
1 tablespoon curry powder
½ teaspoon cinnamon
¼ teaspoon cayenne pepper
⅛ teaspoon nutmeg
2½ pounds sweet potatoes, peeled
   and cut into ½-inch cubes

6 cups reduced-sodium chicken
   broth
½ teaspoon dried thyme
1 small bay leaf
Salt and pepper to taste
½ cup milk
Sour cream and chopped roasted
   peanuts for garnish

In a large pot over medium heat, melt butter. Add ginger, celery, and onion; cook 5–7 minutes until soft. Add curry powder, cinnamon, cayenne, and nutmeg. Cook 1 minute, stirring constantly. Add sweet potatoes, broth, thyme, bay leaf, salt, and pepper. Increase heat to high, and bring to a boil. Lower heat to medium, and simmer 25 minutes or until sweet potatoes are cooked through. Transfer soup in batches to blender or food processor, and purée. Thin soup with milk. Spoon into bowls, and garnish with a dollop of sour cream and chopped peanuts. Serves 12.

*May substitute 1 teaspoon dry ground ginger.

North Carolina Cook Book (North Carolina)

Editor's Extra: Raw sweet potatoes are hard to peel and chop. Okay to bake or boil unpeeled potatoes till soft. Now they will be easy to peel and mash, and cook in half the time.

Slow-Roasted Onion Soup

A truly southern onion soup—slow is good!

4 medium-size sweet onions
  (Vidalia or Texas)
¼ cup olive oil
2 bay leaves
4 cups chicken stock (or water)
1 cup heavy cream

1 tablespoon unsalted butter
Salt and pepper to taste
Dollop of sour cream and sliced
  chives for garnish
Truffle oil for garnish

Slice onions; put on baking sheet, and sprinkle with olive oil. Bake in oven at 325° for 20 minutes. Place onions in stockpot over medium heat; caramelize for 15 minutes. Add bay leaves and chicken stock, and simmer 30–40 minutes. Remove bay leaves. Mix soup in a blender; add heavy cream and butter. Purée and strain. Add salt and pepper to taste. Garnish with a dollop of sour cream and chives, and drizzle with truffle oil. Serves 6.

Fine Dining Georgia Style (Georgia)

Editor's Extra: Truffle oil is created when truffles are soaked in olive oil. Available in most gourmet stores, a few drops of truffle oil will give the final touch of class to an unforgettable meal. (But also great without it.)

Bacon and Potato Soup

Crazy good.

8 slices bacon, fried crisp
1 cup chopped onions
2 cups cubed potatoes
1 cup water
1 (10¾-ounce) can cream of
    chicken soup

½ (8-ounce) carton sour cream
1¾ cups milk
½ teaspoon salt
Pepper to taste
2 tablespoons chopped fresh
    parsley

In bacon grease, sauté onions 2–3 minutes. Drain. In a pot with sautéed onions, add potatoes and water; bring to a boil. Cover, and simmer about 15 minutes, or until potatoes are tender. Stir in soup, sour cream, and crumbled bacon. Add milk, salt, pepper, and parsley. Heat to serving temperature. Do not boil. Serves 6.

Kentucky Kitchens Volume I (Kentucky)

Potato Cheese Soup

⅓ cup chopped celery
⅓ cup chopped onion
2 tablespoons butter
4 cups pared and diced potatoes
3 cups chicken broth
2 cups milk
1½ teaspoons salt

Dash of paprika
¼ teaspoon pepper
2 cups shredded sharp Cheddar
  cheese
French fried onion rings or
  croutons for garnish

In large saucepan, sauté celery and onion in butter till tender. Add potatoes and broth. Simmer till potatoes are tender; stir in milk and seasonings; heat through. Add cheese, stirring till melted. Garnish. Yields 7½ cups.

Tennessee's 95 Magic Mixes: Second Helping (Tennessee)

Broccoli Cream Cheese Soup

½ cup chopped green onions
2 tablespoons butter
2 (8-ounce) packages cream
  cheese, cubed
2 cups half-and-half
2 cups chicken broth
3 (10-ounce) packages frozen
  chopped broccoli

1 teaspoon lemon juice
1 teaspoon salt
½ teaspoon black pepper
4 chicken breasts, cooked, boned,
  and cubed (optional)
Parsley and toasted almonds
  for garnish

Sauté onions in butter in large saucepan. Add cream cheese, half-and-half, and broth. In separate saucepan, cook broccoli according to package directions, then drain. Add broccoli, lemon juice, salt, and pepper to broth mixture. You may add chicken at this time, if desired, and heat thoroughly. Garnish with almonds and parsley. Serves 10.

A River's Course (North Carolina)

Red Pepper Bisque

8 red bell peppers
2 yellow onions, chopped
¼ cup butter (½ stick)
2 teaspoons minced garlic
½ cup minced basil leaves

6 cups rich chicken stock,
  divided
2 cups heavy cream
Salt and pepper to taste

Seed red peppers, and cut into 1-inch pieces. Cook red peppers and onions in butter in a large skillet or saucepan over medium heat until onions are translucent, stirring frequently. Add garlic, basil, and 2 cups chicken stock. Simmer about 10 minutes or until red peppers are tender, stirring occasionally. Process mixture in batches in blender or food processor until smooth. Strain into a soup pot, and blend in remaining chicken stock. Simmer 10–15 minutes or until slightly thickened, stirring occasionally. Blend in heavy cream gradually. Add salt and pepper. Heat to serving temperature; do not boil. Ladle into soup bowls. Yields 2½ quarts.

Celebrations (Alabama)

Rappahannock Crab Bisque

1 stick butter or margarine
3 leeks (white part only), washed,
  halved, thinly sliced
1 garlic clove, minced
½ cup all-purpose flour
4 cups chicken broth
½ cup dry white wine
2 cups half-and-half
½ pound fresh crabmeat
¼ teaspoon salt
¼ teaspoon black pepper
Sliced leeks for garnish (white
  part only)

In a large saucepan, melt butter; sauté leeks and garlic over medium-high heat 3 minutes or until tender, stirring constantly. Blend in flour, and cook 1 minute, stirring constantly. Gradually add broth and wine; cook over medium heat, stirring constantly until mixture thickens. Stir in half-and-half, crabmeat, salt, and pepper. Heat thoroughly. Serve garnished with sliced leeks. Yields 6–8 servings.

Very Virginia (Virginia)

Okra and Seafood Gumbo

⅓ pound smoked sausage, sliced
3 tablespoons bacon or pork
   drippings, divided
1 cup diced ham
3 large onions, chopped
3 cloves garlic
3–4 shallots, chopped
2 pounds fresh okra, sliced,
   or 2 (10-ounce) boxes frozen
   okra
3 tablespoons chopped celery
3 tablespoons chopped parsley
1 medium green bell pepper,
   chopped

1 tablespoon Worcestershire
1 (14½-ounce) can stewed or diced
   tomatoes
2 bay leaves
1 teaspoon black pepper
½ teaspoon red pepper
3 quarts hot water
⅓ cup all-purpose flour
¼ cup bacon fat, shortening, or
   vegetable oil
2 cups cold water
3–4 fresh crabs, cleaned
1 pound shrimp, cleaned
½ lemon, sliced

In large heavy pot, fry sausage in half the bacon fat or drippings. Add ham; fry a few minutes longer. Remove meat; fry onions, garlic, and shallots for a few minutes, then add sliced okra and fry well. Do not burn. Add celery, parsley, green bell pepper, and Worcestershire. Add tomatoes, bay leaves, seasoning, ham, and smoked sausage. Let cook a few minutes; add about 3 quarts of hot water. Cook 30 minutes.

Brown flour in remaining bacon fat until dark brown; remove from heat, and stir in 2 cups cold water; add to pot. Stir and cook 20 minutes. Add crabs, shrimp, and lemon slices. Cook until thick as gravy. Serve with cooked rice. (More water may be added for right consistency.) Serves 10.

My Mother Cooked My Way Through Harvard with These Creole Recipes
(Mississippi)

Cool Benedictine Soup

3 medium cucumbers
3 cups chicken broth
2 cups sour cream
3 tablespoons white wine vinegar

2 teaspoons garlic salt
Several drops green food coloring
Chopped almonds for garnish

Peel cucumbers and cut into chunks. Pureé in food processor. Combine with chicken broth, sour cream, vinegar, and seasonings; tint a light green with food coloring. Chill. Serve cold, topped with almonds. Serves 6.

Fillies Flavours (Kentucky)

Georgia Peanut Soup

1 shallot, chopped
2 ribs celery, chopped
2 teaspoons butter or margarine
1 tablespoon all-purpose flour
1 cup chicken stock, divided
3 tablespoons smooth, salt-free
    peanut butter, made from
    freshly ground peanuts

½ cup low-fat milk
½ cup water
2 tablespoons crushed, salt-free
    Georgia peanuts

Sauté shallot and celery in melted butter in a medium skillet for 5 minutes. Add flour, tossing to coat well. Stir in ½ cup chicken stock; simmer 5 minutes. Add remaining ½ cup chicken stock; simmer 5 minutes longer. Strain, separating liquid from vegetables. Blend peanut butter into reserved liquid in a saucepan. Stir in milk.

Combine ¾ cup stock mixture with reserved vegetables in a blender or food processor; process until smooth; stir into saucepan. Cook until heated through, adding water as needed for desired consistency. Serve hot or cold, topped with crushed peanuts. Serves 4.

True Grits (Georgia)

Old Mill Corn Chowder

1 medium red bell pepper, chopped
1 medium yellow bell pepper, chopped
1 tablespoon margarine
Salt and freshly ground white pepper to taste
2 cups water
2 cups chicken broth
3 cups diced potatoes
2 cups diced onions
¾ cup crushed unsalted oyster crackers
2 cups half-and-half
2 cups frozen corn

Sauté peppers in margarine. Add salt and pepper to taste. Set aside. Mix water, broth, potatoes, and onions in saucepan. Cook on medium heat until done. Add cracker crumbs and pepper mixture to potato mixture. Mix well; bring to a boil, then add cream and corn. Simmer 15–20 minutes. Serves 8–10.

A Taste of Heaven (Kentucky)

Sinfully Rich Oyster Stew

4–6 tablespoons butter
1 cup milk
2 cups heavy cream
1½ pints oysters and liquor

Salt, fresh ground black pepper,
    and cayenne pepper to taste
Chopped parsley or paprika

Heat bowls, and add 1 tablespoon butter to each. Keep bowls hot. Heat milk, cream, and oyster liquor to the boiling point. Add oysters, and again bring to boiling point. Season with salt, pepper, and cayenne. Ladle into hot bowls, and garnish with a little chopped parsley or paprika. Serves 4–6.

The Rappahannock Seafood Cookbook (Virginia)

Blues Brothers World-Famous Brunswick Stew

Not sure what the Blues Brothers had to do with it, but this recipe is really good! Feeds a crowd.

4 pounds boneless chicken breasts,
    cut in bite-size pieces
1 pound onions, chopped
2 teaspoons margarine
3 pounds potatoes, cubed
2 (15-ounce) cans corn, drained
1 (15-ounce) can green
    beans, drained

1 (15-ounce) can baby lima beans,
    drained
2 (10¾-ounce) cans tomato soup
1 pound minced pork barbecue
2 teaspoons black pepper
2 teaspoons Tabasco
¼–½ teaspoon red pepper

Sauté chicken and onions in margarine. In a big pot, boil potatoes until semi-soft in just enough water to cover. Put vegetables, soup, barbecue, chicken, and onions into pot with potatoes that have been drained. Add spices, stir, and simmer until hot. Serves 10–12.

A Taste of the Outer Banks II (North Carolina)

E-Z Chili

Your family will think you slaved over the stove.

3 pounds ground beef (more
  or less)
2 packages chili seasoning
1 (15-ounce) can tomato sauce

3 (15-ounce) cans chili beans
  (drain 2 cans, reserve juice)
2 (15-ounce) cans pinto beans,
  drained

Brown beef in a heavy 5-quart pot. Drain. Mix in chili seasoning, and stir well. Add tomato sauce. Add beans, stirring after each can. Depending on how much beef you use, you may need to leave out a can or two. If it is too thick, you can add reserved bean juice (remember this will make it a little hotter), or you can add a small can of tomato sauce. Chili should be thick. Serves 8 or more.

Note: It can be frozen, if you have any leftovers.

Our Favorite Recipes, Volume II (Alabama)

Editor's Extra: For color and extra taste, we added sprinkles of chopped green and white onions, and some shredded Cheddar cheese.

Venison Chili

Got a hunter in the family? If not, substitute ground beef.

Nonstick cooking spray
1 tablespoon olive oil
2 pounds ground or shredded
    venison
2½ cups chopped onion
2 cloves garlic, minced
2 (¾-ounce) packages chili
    seasoning mix, prepared
1 tablespoon steak sauce
1 teaspoon black pepper
1 teaspoon crushed red pepper
    flakes

2 tablespoons chili powder
1 (18-ounce) can tomato juice
2 (16-ounce) cans pinto beans,
    drained
2 teaspoons dried, crumbled basil
1 teaspoon dried, crumbled
    oregano
1 packet sugar substitute
1 (8-ounce) can mushrooms,
    drained
1 large green bell pepper, julienned

Coat bottom of an iron pot with cooking spray; add oil and place over medium-high heat until hot. Brown venison, onion, and garlic until venison is no longer pink and vegetables are opaque. Stir in chili seasoning mix; stir well. Add steak sauce and next 4 ingredients; reduce heat, cover, and simmer 1 hour. Stir occasionally from bottom. Add beans and remaining ingredients; cook, uncovered, an additional 30–40 minutes.

May top with chopped onion and reduced-fat Cheddar; if used, remember to add the additional calories and fat. Yields 9 servings.

Nutritional information per serving: 285.2 cal; 5.1g fat; 33.5g prot; 24.7g carbo; 1024.6mg sod.

Game Gourmet (Mississippi)

Salads

Rainbow Cole Slaw

2 cups shredded green cabbage
1 cup shredded red cabbage
1 carrot, grated
⅓ cup finely chopped onion
⅓ cup finely chopped green
  bell pepper
¼ cup finely chopped sweet
  red bell pepper
1 tablespoon chopped fresh
  parsley
1 cup diced red apple, unpeeled
½ cup sour cream
½ cup mayonnaise
2 teaspoons sugar
1 teaspoon cider vinegar
Salt and pepper to taste

Combine all vegetables, parsley, and apple. In a separate bowl, whip together remaining ingredients. Pour over vegetables, and mix gently. Cover, and refrigerate until chilled. Mix gently before serving. Serves 6 or more.

Kentucky Kitchens Volume I (Kentucky)

Tomato Aspic with Cream Cheese

2 tablespoons unflavored gelatin
¼ cup cold water
1 (10¾-ounce) can tomato soup
2 (3-ounce) packages cream
  cheese
1 cup chopped celery
¼ teaspoon Worcestershire
1 large (7¾-ounce) bottle sliced
  stuffed olives
¼ teaspoon black pepper
2 tablespoons tarragon vinegar
1 cup finely chopped nuts
  (optional)

Dissolve gelatin in cold water. Heat soup to boiling point; add cream cheese, and stir till dissolved. Add gelatin, and let stand till it begins to congeal. Add remaining ingredients, and pour into wet individual molds. Let stand in refrigerator overnight. Serves 8.

The South Carolina Cook Book (South Carolina)

Kum-Back Salad Dressing

1 teaspoon mustard
2 cloves garlic, minced
Dash of Tabasco
Juice of 1 lemon
1 pint mayonnaise

1 tablespoon Worcestershire
Dash of paprika
1 (12-ounce) bottle chili sauce
1 teaspoon black pepper
¼ onion, grated

Mix all ingredients together with electric mixer, and chill. Serve over tossed green salad. Yields about 1½ pints.

Calling All Cooks (Alabama)

Marinated Vegetable Salad

This makes a colorful salad.

¾ cup white vinegar	1 (16-ounce) can green beans
½ cup cooking oil	1 (16-ounce) can whole-kernel corn
1 cup sugar	1 cup finely chopped green bell
1 teaspoon salt	pepper
1 teaspoon pepper	1 cup chopped onion
1 tablespoon water	1 cup chopped celery
1 (16-ounce) can green peas	1 (4-ounce) jar chopped pimentos

In a saucepan, bring to a boil the vinegar, oil, sugar, salt, pepper, and water. Remove from heat, and allow to cool. Drain peas, beans, and corn. Add to pepper, onion, celery, and pimentos; mix well. Pour cooled mixture over vegetables, and stir; marinate at least 4 hours, but preferably overnight.

Drain or use a slotted spoon to serve. Yields 8 cups.

Note: You may use either white or yellow corn.

Mountain Laurel Encore (Kentucky)

Corn Salad

Good with barbeque, hamburgers, or stuffed in a tomato.

2 (12-ounce) cans shoe peg
  corn, drained
2 tomatoes, seeded, drained,
  and chopped, but not peeled
1 bell pepper, seeded and
  chopped
1 purple onion, chopped
1 cucumber, peeled, seeded,
  and chopped

½ cup sour cream
4 tablespoons mayonnaise
2 tablespoons white vinegar
½ teaspoon celery seed
½ teaspoon dry mustard
½ teaspoon black pepper
2 teaspoons salt

Mix all vegetables. Combine sour cream, mayonnaise, vinegar, and seasonings. Pour over vegetables. Cover, and refrigerate overnight. Recipe can easily be doubled. Serves 10–12.

Note: May use a pint of cherry tomatoes, cut in half, in place of regular tomatoes.

Magic (Alabama)

Cornbread Salad

CRUMB MIXTURE:

1 (8½-ounce) package Jiffy
   cornbread mix

1 egg
⅓ cup milk

Combine all, and stir well. Pour into greased 8-inch pan. Bake at 400°
for 15–20 minutes. Cool, and crumble; set aside.

TOMATO MIXTURE:

4 medium tomatoes, peeled and
   chopped
1 green bell pepper, chopped
1 medium onion, chopped

½ cup chopped sweet pickles
9 slices bacon, cooked and
   crumbled

Toss gently. Mix, and set aside.

MAYONNAISE MIXTURE:

1¼ cups mayonnaise

⅓ cup pickle juice

Mix, and set aside.

   Layer ½ Crumb Mixture, ½ Tomato Mixture, and ½ Mayonnaise
Mixture. Repeat. Let set at least 2 hours. Keep refrigerated. Serves 6.

Windsor Academy Cookbook (Georgia)

Appalachian Potato Salad

Appalachian Potato Salad is smooth, creamy, and partly mashed. For the best results, most mountaineers know to use mature—not new— Idaho or Kennebec baking potatoes, and mix the salad when the potatoes are hot. Do not allow them to sit after cooking.

4 medium-size potatoes
4 eggs

½ cup diced pickles, relish, or pimentos

Cut potatoes in half lengthwise. Boil 30 minutes, or until soft to the center (or, do as I do—place them in a pressure cooker, add 1 cup water, and cook 15–20 minutes after the pressure is up).

While potatoes are cooking, boil eggs 10 minutes. Run them under cold water, and peel shells. Mash eggs. Stir in pickles.

When potatoes are cooked, run them under cold water, and while they're still hot, pull off skins. Remove and discard dark spots and blemishes.

DRESSING:
½ cup safflower oil
¾ cup mayonnaise
2 tablespoons red wine vinegar

2 teaspoons Dijon-style mustard
1½ teaspoons salt
1 teaspoon dill weed

In a large mixing bowl, whisk together Dressing ingredients. Stir in eggs and pickles. Dice hot potatoes, and stir them in. Refrigerate until ready to serve. Serves 8.

Healthy Choice Alternative: Instead of this Dressing, use a generous amount of a store-bought thick, light, low-calorie, fat-free, and cholesterol-free dressing.

Mountain Country Cooking (Kentucky)

Cheese Puffs with Chicken Salad

4 tablespoons butter
½ cup boiling water
½ cup all-purpose flour

Dash of salt
2 eggs
½ cup shredded Swiss cheese

Melt butter in boiling water. Add ¼ cup flour and a dash of salt. Stir rapidly until mixture leaves sides of pan and forms a ball that does not separate. Remove from heat and cool slightly. Add egg and beat until smooth. Stir in shredded cheese. Drop from a teaspoon onto a greased baking sheet, and bake in a 400° oven for 20 minutes. Cool, and split. Fill with chicken salad. Unfilled puffs may be kept in freezer.

PARTY CHICKEN SALAD:

2 cups chopped, cooked chicken
¼ cup minced celery
2 tablespoons minced green
    onion
2 tablespoons minced pimentos
2 tablespoons white wine

¼ cup mayonnaise
½ teaspoon salt
Dash of pepper
¼ teaspoon lemon juice
¼ cup sliced almonds

Mix chicken with celery, green onion, pimentos, wine, mayonnaise, salt, pepper, lemon juice, and sliced almonds. Fill puffs with chicken salad. Yields 10–12.

The Alabama Heritage Cookbook (Alabama)

Shrimp Salad

3½ cups cooked, peeled, and
  deveined shrimp
1 cup chopped celery
⅓ cup finely chopped onion
1 cup chopped green bell pepper
2 hard-boiled eggs, chopped
¼ cup fresh lime juice

2 tablespoons ketchup
2 teaspoons sugar
1 teaspoon Worcestershire
½ teaspoon salt
1 teaspoon Tabasco, or to taste
¾ cup real mayonnaise, not
  salad dressing

In a 2-quart mixing bowl, combine shrimp, celery, onion, green pepper, and eggs; pour lime juice over all. In a small bowl, combine remaining ingredients, except mayonnaise. Pour over shrimp, and stir. Add mayonnaise, and blend well. Chill; serve on lettuce. Serves 6–8.

Note: Shrimp may be cut into bite-size pieces.

Tropical Tastes and Tantalizing Tales (Florida)

Marinated Shrimp

A super salad on a bed of lettuce, and equally great as an hors d'oeuvre.

4 pounds medium shrimp,
   boiled, shelled, and deveined
4 onions, sliced and ringed
4 lemons, thinly sliced
Juice of 1 lemon
1 cup condensed tomato soup
1½ cups vegetable oil
¾ cup white vinegar

¼ cup sugar
½ teaspoon paprika
1 teaspoon cayenne
1 tablespoon dry mustard
1 tablespoon Worcestershire
2 teaspoons salt
¼ teaspoon Tabasco

Place shrimp, onions, and lemons in large container. Mix remaining ingredients together. Pour over shrimp mixture. Marinate in refrigerator at least 24 hours.

Serve in a bowl in marinade with toothpicks, or drain and serve as a salad on a bed of lettuce.

Tea-Time at the Masters® (Georgia)

Orange-Avocado Toss

1 medium head lettuce, torn
   into bite-size pieces
1 small cucumber, thinly sliced
2 tablespoons green onions, sliced

1 avocado, seeded, peeled, sliced
1 (11-ounce) can Mandarin
   oranges, drained

In a large salad bowl, combine ingredients.

DRESSING:
¼ cup orange juice
½ cup oil
2 tablespoons sugar

2 tablespoons red wine vinegar
1 tablespoon lemon juice
¼ teaspoon salt

In a screw-top jar, combine Dressing ingredients. Cover tightly and shake well. Just before serving, pour over salad. Toss lightly. Serves 8.

Out of Our League (North Carolina)

Holiday Pasta Salad

This looks like a lot of ingredients and a lot of trouble, but you can have the salad made in approximately 30 minutes. And besides, it is worth all the time and effort you put into it. Everyone loves this salad.

½ cup tarragon vinegar
1 (9-ounce) jar green olives, whole, drained and liquid reserved
¼ cup oil

1 clove garlic, minced
1 teaspoon oregano
3 (6-ounce) jars sliced mushrooms, drained

Mix vinegar, olive liquid, oil, garlic, and oregano; add mushrooms and olives. Marinate overnight, if possible.

2 cups Newman's Own Oil and Vinegar Salad Dressing

2 cups ranch dressing (regular, not light)

Mix well, and reserve for salad. (If you should have any left over, the combination of these 2 dressings makes a great salad dressing.)

1 (8-ounce) package pasta (your choice, but colored, if possible)
1 medium red bell pepper, diced
1 medium green bell pepper, diced
1 medium sweet onion, thinly sliced (optional)

1 cup frozen small English peas, uncooked
1 (2-ounce) jar chopped pimentos, drained
½ (12-ounce) jar mild banana pepper rings

Cook pasta according to directions on package, but do not overcook. Drain and rinse. Add remaining ingredients; stir until completely mixed. Add marinade and salad dressing. This will keep in refrigerator for about 2 weeks, but won't last that long if you have many pasta lovers.

Variation: Grilled chicken or baked ham can be added to your pasta salad to make it a meal.

Christmas Memories (Florida)

Vegetables & Sides

Fried Green Tomatoes with Rémoulade

2 medium green tomatoes
1 tablespoon salt, divided
1 tablespoon freshly cracked
  black pepper, divided
2 cups panko (Japanese
  bread crumbs)
2 tablespoons paprika
1 cup chopped fresh parsley
4 eggs, beaten well
2 cups all-purpose flour
2 cups vegetable oil

Slice tomatoes and sprinkle with salt and pepper. Combine panko, paprika, parsley, and remaining salt and pepper. Beat eggs in separate bowl, and put flour in another. Dip tomatoes into flour, shaking off excess—this is very important; dip into egg, letting excess drip off. Press tomatoes into bread crumbs, thoroughly coating both sides. Heat oil in skillet. When oil is hot, add tomatoes, frying over medium heat. Cook until golden on both sides. Drain on paper towels. Drizzle with Rémoulade, and serve with a fresh lemon slice. Serves 8.

RÉMOULADE:
¼ cup ketchup
1 cup mayonnaise
¼ cup chopped fresh parsley
2 teaspoons hot pepper sauce
1 medium shallot
2 tablespoons capers
2 teaspoons vinegar
1 tablespoon paprika
2 teaspoons lemon juice

Combine all ingredients in food processor. Blend until smooth. Refrigerate for 2 hours.

Fine Dining Georgia Style (Georgia)

Fried Green Tomato Casserole

Not actually fried, this is a delicious use of green tomatoes.

6 medium green tomatoes,
   sliced in rounds
Salt and pepper to taste
1 cup Ritz Cracker crumbs,
   divided

1 cup grated sharp Cheddar
   cheese, divided
6 tablespoons butter, divided

Layer half the tomatoes in a greased shallow dish. Sprinkle with salt and pepper. Add ½ cup cracker crumbs and ½ cup cheese. Dot with 3 tablespoons butter (in small pieces). Layer remaining tomatoes; add seasonings and remaining ½ cup cheese. Add remaining ½ cup crumbs and 3 tablespoons butter. Bake, covered, at 350° for 30 minutes. Uncover, and bake 10 minutes or until brown. Serves 6.

Aliant Cooks for Education (Alabama)

Tomato Pie

1 medium onion, chopped
1 medium tomato, diced
1 (9-inch) deep-dish pie shell,
    baked
1 pound bacon, cooked

1 cup shredded mozzarella
    cheese
1 cup shredded Cheddar cheese
1 cup Miracle Whip Salad
    Dressing

Preheat oven to 350°. Layer onion and tomato in pie shell; crumble bacon on top. In a medium mixing bowl, mix cheeses and salad dressing together. Pour cheese mixture into pie shell, covering all the bacon and spreading to edges. Bake at 350° until cheese melts and is golden brown. Serve hot or cold. Serves 6–8.

Kentucky Cook Book (Kentucky)

Granny Greenes' Okra and Tomatoes

A 1930's depression dish.

1 large onion, chopped
2 pounds fresh okra, cut up
5 or 6 large tomatoes, cut up, or
    2 (28-ounce) cans tomatoes,
    drained

Salt and pepper to taste

Sauté onion in small amount of oil. Add okra; cook about 10 minutes. Add tomatoes according to desired amount. Stir, and simmer until okra is done. Season to taste. A very small amount of plain flour may be added for extra thickness, if desired. Either flour okra before adding to onions or add flour while okra and tomatoes are simmering. Serve with pone of hot cornbread. Serves 8 or more.

Calling All Cooks (Alabama)

Green Beans Wrapped in Bacon

3 (15-ounce) cans whole green
   beans, drained
1 pound bacon

1 cup brown sugar
½ cup vinegar
Salt and pepper to taste

Put 8–10 beans together in a bundle, and wrap with a strip of bacon. Secure with a toothpick. Place bundles in a casserole dish. Mix brown sugar, vinegar, and seasonings together. Pour mixture over beans, and bake about 50 minutes at 350°. Yields 12–14 bundles.

Recipes from the Heart of Branch (Mississippi)

Lima Bean and Corn Casserole Supreme

1½ cups milk
½ cup butter
½ teaspoon salt
¼ teaspoon pepper
¼ cup all-purpose flour
2 cups cooked lima beans

¼ cup grated Parmesan cheese
1 small onion, chopped
¼ cup chopped pimentos
2 cups whole-kernel corn
½ cup bread crumbs
1 tablespoon butter, melted

Make white sauce using the first 5 ingredients. Cook 3 minutes after it thickens. Add remaining ingredients, except bread crumbs and melted butter. Pour into a lightly greased casserole dish, and top with buttered bread crumbs. Bake at 350° for 30 minutes. Serves 8.

Mama's Recipes (North Carolina)

Corn Maque Choux

This is one of the choice corn dishes in southwest Louisiana. Handed down from the Indians, the flavor is outstanding.

4 tablespoons bacon fat or butter	1 teaspoon cayenne pepper
8 cups fresh off the cob sweet corn, or frozen, divided	½ teaspoon garlic powder
	1 bay leaf
1 cup fresh or canned whole tomatoes	1 teaspoon black pepper
	1 cup chicken stock or chicken bouillon
2 cups finely chopped onions	1 cup milk
1 cup finely chopped bell pepper	1 teaspoon sugar
	1 teaspoon basil

Melt bacon fat or butter in 6-quart iron pot. Add one cup corn, and parch to a medium brown (do not burn), about 10 minutes. Strain, and set aside. Reserve 1 cup. Add to the drippings all vegetables except corn. Cook on high heat for 10 minutes. Stir frequently to keep from sticking or burning. Add corn and all other ingredients except chicken stock, milk, sugar, and basil. Set aside cup of browned corn. Stir well, and cook at high heat, covered, for 5 minutes. Uncover, scrape corn crust from bottom of pot, and cook for 5 minutes, continuing to stir crust from bottom to prevent burning. Remove bay leaf, add browned corn, and continue to cook on high heat for about 10 minutes. Continue to scrape and mix crust formed at the bottom of the pot.

Now add chicken stock, milk, and sugar. Cover, and simmer on low heat for 15 minutes. If corn is a little dry, add more milk; add basil. Adjust seasoning as needed, and simmer for 5 more minutes. Stir occasionally. Serves 10.

Cajun Men Cook (Louisiana)

Fresh Corn Pudding

3 cups fresh corn, cut from cob
6 whole eggs, stirred well
  (not beaten)
3 cups heavy cream
½ cup sugar
1 teaspoon salt
1 teaspoon all-purpose flour
½ teaspoon baking powder
2 teaspoons butter, melted

Using a sharp paring knife, barely cut through tips of corn kernels, then scrape cob to remove remaining juice and pulp. Stir in eggs and cream. Combine dry ingredients and add to corn mixture; stir in melted butter, and mix well. Pour into greased baking dish, and bake at 350° about 1 hour, until knife inserted in center comes out clean. Serves 8.

Bluegrass Winners (Kentucky)

Country Corn Relish

1 tablespoon cornstarch
1 teaspoon turmeric
1 cup plus 1 tablespoon vinegar,
  divided
2 green bell peppers, seeded
  and diced
2 sweet red bell peppers, seeded
  and diced
½ pound white onions, diced
1 large cucumber, peeled and
  diced
2 large tomatoes, peeled and
  diced
2 ears fresh corn, cut from cob
4 stalks celery, diced
1¼ cups sugar
¼ teaspoon mustard seed

In large kettle or pot, blend cornstarch and turmeric with 1 tablespoon vinegar. Add remaining 1 cup vinegar, and mix in all the other ingredients. Bring to a boil, then reduce heat and simmer, uncovered, for 50–60 minutes, or until thick. Pour into hot sterilized jars, and seal. (Relish may also be cooled and poured into refrigerator or freezer containers. Refrigerate for immediate use or freeze for future serving.) Yields 1½ quarts.

Apron Strings (Virginia)

Creole Corn

1 (10-ounce) package frozen
   whole-kernel corn
½ cup chopped bell pepper
⅓ cup chopped celery
¼ cup chopped onion
1 tablespoon vegetable oil
1 (8-ounce) can tomato sauce

1 (4½-ounce) jar sliced
   mushrooms, drained
1 tablespoon chili sauce
1 teaspoon brown sugar
⅛ teaspoon garlic powder
1 small tomato, chopped
Dash of Tabasco

Cook corn according to directions. Drain. In medium skillet, sauté pepper, celery, and onion in oil until tender. Stir in corn. Add remaining ingredients. Cook until mixture comes to a boil. Continue cooking for 5 minutes. Serves 4–5.

Nibbles Cooks Cajun (Arkansas)

Mom's Marinated Carrots

5 cups peeled and sliced carrots
1 medium onion, chopped
1 small green bell pepper,
　chopped
1 (10¾-ounce) can tomato soup
½ cup oil

1 cup sugar
¾ cup red wine vinegar
1 teaspoon mustard
1 teaspoon Worcestershire
Salt and pepper to taste

Cook carrots in steamer basket over 1-inch boiling water in covered saucepan 7–8 minutes, until just tender. Mix all other ingredients together in large bowl, and add carrots. Refrigerate overnight in airtight container. Serve cold.

Paris Winners (Kentucky)

Candied Carrots

1 pound carrots, peeled and
　steamed

1 cup peach preserves
¼ cup butter, melted

Cut carrots in slices. Add peach preserves and butter in shallow pan. Bake for 30 minutes at 325°. Serves 6.

A Samford Celebration Cookbook (Alabama)

Onion Fries

¾ cup self-rising flour
½ teaspoon baking powder
1 tablespoon cornmeal
½ cup non-fat dry milk

2 teaspoons sugar
½ teaspoon salt
2½ cups chopped onions
½ cup water (more or less)

Combine all ingredients, except onions. Add cold water (about ½ cup), a little at a time, until you have a very thick batter. Add onions, and mix well. Make small half-dollar size patties by dripping from spoon into hot shallow oil and flattening slightly with back of spoon. Brown on both sides. Yields about 30.

The Farmer's Daughters (Arkansas)

Baked Stuffed Onions

May be made the day before, refrigerated, and baked before serving.

6 large onions, peeled
3 tablespoons butter
¼ cup dry bread crumbs
¼ cup chopped pecans

Salt and pepper to taste
1½ cups grated sharp cheese,
  divided
Paprika

Choose onions that are uniform in size. Cook in boiling salted water 25–30 minutes, or till tender, but not soft. Drain; cool.

Carefully scoop out centers. Chop, and sauté in butter till golden; cool. Add bread crumbs, pecans, salt, pepper, and part of the cheese. When ready to bake, preheat oven to 350°. Grease shallow baking dish. Place onions in baking dish. Top with remaining cheese. Sprinkle with paprika. Bake about 15 minutes, or till cheese is melted and slightly brown. Yields 6 servings.

Minnie Pearl Cooks (Tennessee)

Stuffed Eggplant

4 medium eggplants
1 cup finely chopped onions
½ cup finely chopped celery
¼ pound margarine
12 stale saltine crackers
2 eggs

2 pounds boiled shrimp, peeled
  and deveined
1 pound white crabmeat
Parsley and green onions
Italian bread crumbs

Cut each eggplant into 2 equal parts; remove middle and chop (save shells). Sauté onions and celery in margarine; add chopped eggplant; smother until done. Crush crackers, and put in bowl with eggs. Mix well with chopped boiled shrimp, smothered eggplant, crabmeat, parsley, and green onions. Season to taste. Boil shells of eggplant for 10 minutes, or until tender; then stuff with mixture. Top each eggplant with Italian bread crumbs. Bake 20–25 minutes at 350°. Serves 8.

Secrets of The Original Don's Seafood & Steakhouse (Louisiana)

Souffléd Squash

This recipe was a specialty of Allison's Wells in its day.

2 eggs, separated
2–3 medium crookneck squash
¼ cup finely chopped celery
⅛ cup finely chopped green
   bell pepper
¼ cup finely chopped onion
1 teaspoon sugar

1 teaspoon baking powder
1 tablespoon all-purpose flour
⅔ cup milk
Salt and pepper to taste
⅓ cup cracker crumbs
3 tablespoons margarine

Beat egg yolks and whites separately, adding 1 tablespoon of water to each (beat egg whites stiff). Slice squash, and cook in small amount of water until tender. Mash squash; drain. Add celery, green pepper, onion, sugar, baking powder, flour, milk, salt, and pepper. Add egg yolks and whites separately. Pour into greased glass or aluminum cups; top with cracker crumbs, and dot with margarine . Place in a large baking pan. Bake in 350° oven until lightly brown, about 20 minutes. Top with grated cheese, if desired. Serves 8 generously.

Madison County Cookery (Mississippi)

Squash Dressing

8 yellow squash, chopped
1 onion, chopped
1 bell pepper, chopped
2 tablespoons butter
1 (7-ounce) package Mexican
  cornbread mix

1 (10¾-ounce) can cream of
  mushroom soup
½ pound Velveeta cheese, cubed
1 (2-ounce) jar pimentos

Sauté vegetables in butter in large skillet. Cook cornbread per package directions; cool, crumble, and mix with vegetables. Add soup, cheese, and pimentos; heat till blended. Pour into greased casserole dish, and bake in 350° oven for 20–30 minutes until bubbly. Serves 6–8.

Family Traditions (Louisiana)

Crustless Spinach Quiche

1 cup chopped onion
1 cup sliced fresh mushrooms
1 tablespoon vegetable oil
1 (10-ounce) package frozen
    chopped spinach, thawed
    and well drained

⅔ cup finely chopped, fully
    cooked ham
5 eggs
3 cups shredded Muenster or
    Monterey Jack cheese
⅛ teaspoon pepper

In a large skillet, sauté onion and mushrooms in oil until tender. Add spinach and ham. Cook and stir until excess moisture is evaporated. Cool slightly. Beat eggs; add cheese, and mix well. Stir in spinach mixture and pepper; blend well. Spread evenly into a greased 9-inch pie plate or quiche dish. Bake at 350° for 40–45 minutes or until knife inserted near center comes out clean. Serves 6.

Treasures from Hope (Kentucky)

Spinach Stuffed Manicotti

1 pound ground meat
1 onion, chopped
1 teaspoon chopped garlic
½ bell pepper, chopped
1 (14 ounce) package frozen
    chopped spinach, thawed
¼ cup cottage cheese

2 eggs, well beaten
14 manicotti shells, cooked
1 (29-ounce) jar spaghetti sauce
½ cup grated Parmesan cheese

1 cup shredded mozzarella
    cheese

Cook ground meat, onion, garlic, and bell pepper; season to taste. Drain well, and set aside to cool. Cook and drain spinach, cool; add cottage cheese and eggs; mix well. Add to meat mixture. Stuff shells with mixture, and place in oiled 9x13-inch pan. Pour spaghetti sauce over manicotti shells. Sprinkle with Parmesan cheese, then sprinkle with mozzarella cheese. Preheat oven to 350°, and bake for 30 minutes. Serves 6–8.

Sisters' Secrets (Louisiana)

Collard Greens

Do not season collards until they have cooked down, as it is very easy to have a heavy hand with the salt and pepper.

3 pounds collard greens, washed,
   chopped
2 cups water
½ pound side meat or ham bone,
   or 1 ham hock

1 tablespoon white vinegar
Salt, pepper, and sugar to taste

Put all ingredients except seasonings into pot; cover, bring to a boil, reduce heat to simmer, and cook 45 minutes; add seasonings, and cook till tender. Serve with hot cornbread. Serves 4.

Southern Vegetable Cooking (South Carolina)

Editor's Extra: In the South, cornbread is a must with any kind of cooked greens. Even better to dunk it in the pot liquor.

Red Potato Strips

1 stick margarine, softened
1 package dry onion soup mix
Black pepper to taste

5–6 red potatoes, scrubbed
and quartered

Combine margarine and soup mix, and spread on peppered potatoes. Put potatoes into a Pam-sprayed casserole dish, and seal with foil. Bake at 350° for 1 hour or until tender. Remove foil, and bake another 10 minutes. Yields 10–12 servings.

Betty is Still "Winking" at Cooking (Arkansas)

Ro-Tel Potatoes

8 medium white potatoes
1 teaspoon salt
3 tablespoons margarine, melted
1 large onion, chopped
1 (4½-ounce) jar sliced mushrooms,
    drained

1 (10-ounce) can Ro-Tel tomatoes
    and diced green chiles
1 pound Velveeta cheese, cubed

In a large saucepan, cook potatoes in jackets in salted, boiling water for 30 minutes or until tender; drain, and set aside to cool. Peel cooled potatoes, and dice. Place in a greased 2-quart baking dish.

Melt margarine in a large skillet over medium heat; sauté onion and mushrooms 3–4 minutes or until tender. Add Ro-Tel tomatoes with juice and cheese. Cook over medium-low heat, stirring constantly, until cheese is melted and smooth. Pour cheese mixture over diced potatoes. Bake, uncovered, at 350° for 25–30 minutes or until bubbly. Serves 8.

Treasured Family Favorites (Mississippi)

Candied Yams

3–4 medium sweet potatoes	Pinch of cinnamon
¾ cup sugar	1–2 tablespoons water
Pinch of nutmeg	1 teaspoon vanilla
Pinch of salt	1 tablespoon butter

Boil sweet potatoes until done. Peel, slice, and place in buttered glass baking dish. In saucepan, combine sugar, nutmeg, salt, and cinnamon. Add sufficient water to moisten. Simmer 3 minutes. Add vanilla. Dot potatoes with butter, and pour sauce over potatoes. Bake at 350° for 20 minutes. Serves 6.

Secret Recipes (North Carolina)

Sweet Potato Soufflé

A delicious side dish . . . or a dessert.

POTATOES:

3 cups sweet potatoes, cooked and mashed, or 1 (29-ounce) can sweet potatoes, drained	1 teaspoon vanilla
	½ cup milk
	½ cup butter, melted
1 cup sugar	1 teaspoon vanilla (optional)
2 eggs, well beaten	

Mix potato ingredients together until well blended, and spread in a 9x13-inch pan.

TOPPING:

1 cup light brown sugar	1 cup pecans, chopped
½ cup all-purpose flour	⅓ cup butter, softened

Mix well. Ingredients will be stiff and crumbly. Crumble over top of sweet potatoes. Bake in 350° oven for 30 minutes. Serves 6.

Note: This may also be put into 2 unbaked pie shells, baked 30–40 minutes, and served as a dessert.

Culinary Arts & Crafts (Florida)

Roasted Sweet Potato Wedges

5 pounds sweet potatoes,
   peeled, cut crosswise into
   halves
2 tablespoons olive oil
1 teaspoon salt

½ teaspoon coarsely ground
   pepper
⅔ cup peach preserves
½ teaspoon cinnamon

Combine sweet potatoes, olive oil, salt, and pepper in a large bowl, and toss to coat. Arrange sweet potatoes in a single layer on 2 baking sheets. Roast at 450° on 2 oven racks for 30–40 minutes or until tender. Combine peach preserves and cinnamon in a small bowl, and beat with a wire whisk until blended. Spread evenly over sweet potatoes. Roast 5 minutes longer, or until the glaze is hot and bubbly. Yields 14 servings.

Savor the Spirit (Alabama)

New Year's Black-Eyed Peas

Enough to feed thirty guests splendidly.

3 pounds dried black-eyed peas
2 ribs celery, chopped
3 large onions, chopped
6 large carrots, peeled, chopped
2 large green bell peppers,
    chopped
3 pounds cooked ham, cut into
    bite-size pieces
7 cloves garlic, crushed

4 small red bell peppers, chopped
    (optional)
½ teaspoon thyme
5 bay leaves
2 teaspoons salt
1 teaspoon black pepper
1 teaspoon sugar
Additional salt and black pepper
    to taste

Soak peas in water to cover for 8–10 hours; drain. Place peas in large saucepan. Add celery, onions, carrots, green peppers, ham, garlic, red peppers, thyme, bay leaves, salt, black pepper, and sugar; mix well. Add enough water to cover peas by 2 inches. Bring to a boil over high heat. Reduce heat to low. Cook, covered, 8–10 hours. Season with additional salt and black pepper to taste. Serve with cornbread, turnip greens, and pepper sauce. May serve over rice. Yields 30 servings.

Bay Tables (Alabama)

Hoppin' John

A traditional New Year's Day feast; peas for good luck, "greens" for money.

1 cup dried cowpeas or
   black-eyed peas
1 cup raw rice
½ pound slab bacon, or
   1 ham hock

1 quart cold water
1 teaspoon salt
¼ teaspoon pepper
⅛ teaspoon cayenne pepper
Chopped onion

Wash and soak peas according to package directions. Cook rice according to package directions. Cut bacon or ham hock into small pieces, and fry. Cook peas in 1 quart cold water, adding a little bacon grease. Add salt, pepper, and cayenne. Cook until peas are tender but firm, about 45 minutes. Approximately 1 cup of liquid should remain. Add cooked rice. Heat 2–3 minutes; serve. Garnish with chopped onion and drained bacon or ham. Serves 4–6.

Atlanta Cooknotes (Georgia)

Savannah River Red Rice

1 cup tomato juice
1½ cups chicken broth
2 tablespoons tomato paste
⅛ teaspoon cayenne
½ teaspoon salt
¼ teaspoon white pepper

½ cup chopped onion
½ cup finely chopped celery
¼ cup chopped green bell pepper
6 tablespoons olive oil
2 cups parboiled rice

Combine juice, broth, tomato paste, cayenne, salt, and pepper in a large oven-proof saucepan. Bring to a simmer. Sauté onion, celery, and green pepper in oil in a skillet until tender. Stir in rice, coating with oil. Add rice mixture to tomato mixture; mix well. Bring to a boil. Bake, covered, at 350°, or simmer, covered, for 20–25 minutes. Serves 6.

Variation: May add 4 ounces hot, cooked sausage before baking.

From Black Tie to Blackeyed Peas (Georgia)

Grandma Jo's Famous Mac and Cheese

1 (8-ounce) box macaroni
1 stick butter
1 large egg
2 cups small-curd cottage
   cheese (4% butterfat)

1 cup sour cream
½ cup half-and-half
1 teaspoon salt
2 cups shredded sharp Cheddar
   cheese

Cook macaroni according to directions, then drain and add butter; set aside. Mix egg, cottage cheese, sour cream, half-and-half, and salt. Add macaroni and cheese; mix well, and place in buttered 9x13-inch pan.

TOPPING:
½ stick butter, softened
1 sleeve Ritz Crackers, crushed

1 cup shredded sharp Cheddar
   cheese

Mix all ingredients; spread evenly over top of macaroni and cheese mixture. Bake at 350° for 45 minutes.

Culinary Classics (Georgia)

Poultry

The Best Fried Chicken

5–6 pieces chicken	**Buttermilk**
1 teaspoon salt	**2–3 cups self-rising flour**

When you buy fresh chicken to fry, I recommend immediately skinning and rinsing it well. Place the chicken in an airtight container with water, some ice, and salt. (The amount of salt depends on the amount of chicken. For 5–6 pieces, 1 teaspoon of salt dissolved in water is enough.) When we prepare our chicken this way at the Irondale Cafe, we never add extra salt. Store the chicken in the refrigerator for up to 2 days; drain water, and pour buttermilk over chicken. Return it to the refrigerator until you are ready to fry it.

Sift flour into a large mixing bowl; set aside. Remove cleaned and skinned chicken from refrigerator. Remove from buttermilk and place on platter; let excess buttermilk drain off. Place drained chicken into flour, turning to coat well, patting it on, if necessary.

Heat oil in frying pan or fryer to approximately 350°. Place pieces of chicken in pan (place chicken breasts with the thick side down, bone turned toward center of pan). You may have to turn the heat down some, but remember that the cold chicken will cool the oil, and if the oil is not hot enough, the chicken will absorb the oil and be soggy.

Fry at medium-high heat approximately 7 minutes; turn chicken over; brown other side for 6–7 minutes. Be sure chicken is well done. Fry dark meat as long as white meat because of the larger bones in the leg and thigh.

Note: You may cover the chicken and let it steam for a few minutes, but for crispier chicken, leave it uncovered.

Irondale Cafe Original WhistleStop Cookbook (Alabama)

Annabell's Batter-Fried Chicken

1 egg, beaten
1 cup water
1 cup all-purpose flour
1 teaspoon garlic salt
1 teaspoon savory salt
¼ teaspoon pepper

1 heaping tablespoon baking
  powder
Vegetable oil for deep-frying
1 whole chicken, cut up and
  patted dry

In a bowl, combine egg and water; beat well. Add flour; stir until smooth. Add salts, pepper, and baking powder; blend well. Mixture should foam when baking powder is added. Place oil in a deep pot or deep-fat fryer; heat to 375°. Dip chicken pieces in batter. Deep-fry a few pieces at a time 20–25 minutes, or until browned. Drain on paper towels on wire racks. Keep chicken warm. If chicken is not completely cooked, bake in a preheated 325° oven about 20 minutes. Chicken can be deep-fried in the morning and crisped in the oven for 30 minutes before serving. It can also be frozen, thawed, and crisped. Decant oil after frying, and store for future use. Serves 4.

Atlanta Cooknotes (Georgia)

Quick Chicken and Broccoli Crêpes

1 (10-ounce) package frozen,
  chopped broccoli
1 (10¾-ounce) can cream of
  chicken soup
½ teaspoon Worcestershire
2 cups cooked, chopped chicken

⅔ cup grated Parmesan cheese,
  divided
9–10 crêpes
⅓ cup mayonnaise
1 tablespoon milk

Cook broccoli according to package directions; drain thoroughly. Combine with soup, Worcestershire, chicken, and ⅓ cup cheese. Fill crêpes with chicken mixture; roll up and place in shallow baking pan. Combine mayonnaise with milk; spread over crepes. Sprinkle with remaining ⅓ cup cheese. Broil until bubbly. Yields 9–10 crêpes.

Festival Cookbook (Mississippi)

Poppy Seed Chicken

1 whole chicken
1 (8-ounce) container sour
  cream
1 (10¾-ounce) can cream
  of chicken soup

36 Ritz Crackers (about one
  stack)
½ cup margarine, melted
2 tablespoons poppy seeds

Boil chicken, then skin and debone. Preheat oven to 350°. Place chicken in greased 8x11-inch baking dish. Combine sour cream and soup; pour over chicken. Crush crackers, and mix with margarine and poppy seeds. Sprinkle on top of chicken. Bake 30–35 minutes. Double recipe for 9x13-inch dish. Serve over rice. Yields 6–8 servings.

Collard Greens, Watermelons, and "Miss" Charlotte's Pie
(North Carolina)

Editor's Extra: Buy a rotisserie chicken to save time. If you're intimidated about boiling, skinning, and deboning a chicken, feel free to boil boneless, skinless breasts and/or thighs. Love to freeze the chicken stock to use later.

Chicken Key West

(State Finalist Winner)

¼ pound butter or margarine
1 whole chicken, cut in parts
  and skinned
1 teaspoon salt
1 teaspoon freshly ground pepper

¼ teaspoon paprika
1 large onion, thinly sliced
3–4 cloves garlic, crushed
¼ cup Key lime juice

Melt butter over medium heat in large frying pan with cover. Add chicken and cook until light brown on all sides. Sprinkle with salt, pepper, and paprika. Add onion and garlic. Cook 5 minutes, stirring occasionally. Pour lime juice over chicken. Cover, and simmer 25 minutes or until fork can be inserted with ease. Remove cover, and cook a few minutes until chicken is a golden color.

Margaritaville Cookbook (Florida)

Chicken Tetrazzini for a Crowd

2 (2½–3 pound) whole chickens,
  cut up
Water to cover
Salt and pepper to taste
1 (12-ounce) package spaghetti
1 green bell pepper, chopped
1 onion, chopped

1 stick margarine
⅔ cups all-purpose flour
4 cups milk
1 can cream of mushroom soup
1 pound sharp Cheddar cheese,
  grated (reserve 1 cup for top)

Place chicken pieces in a large boiler; cover with water. Add salt and pepper to taste, cook until tender. Remove from broth. Cool; remove skin and bones. Set chicken aside. Cook spaghetti in chicken broth until tender. In a large skillet or saucepan, sauté pepper and onion in margarine until clear. Add flour, milk, soup, cheese, salt, and pepper to taste. Cook until thickened. Add sauce and chicken to cooked spaghetti. Pour into a large shallow baking dish. Sprinkle top with cheese. Bake at 400° for 30 minutes. Yields 4 quarts. Freezes well.

Hallmark's Collection of Home Tested Recipes (Alabama)

Chicken Spaghetti

1 (2- to 3-pound) whole chicken
Salt and pepper to taste
1 (12-ounce) package spaghetti
1 large onion, chopped

1 stick margarine
½ (16-ounce) block Velveeta
 cheese, cubed
1 (10-ounce) can Ro-Tel tomatoes

Boil chicken in seasoned water until done; reserve broth. Skin, debone, and chop chicken into bite-size pieces. Cook spaghetti in chicken broth.

In separate pan, sauté onion in margarine; add cheese, and stir till melted; add this to drained spaghetti. Mix in chicken and Ro-Tel tomatoes. Bake in 325° oven for 30 minutes, or until heated through.

Bountiful Blessings–DeKalb (Mississippi)

Country Chicken Pie

4 chicken breast halves,
    cooked and deboned
1 small onion
2 ribs celery
1 carrot
1 small potato
6 tablespoons butter or
    margarine

6 tablespoons all-purpose flour
2½ cups milk
2 chicken bouillon cubes
1 teaspoon Worcestershire
1 teaspoon salt
Pepper to taste
Biscuits (about 15)

Boil chicken in enough water to cover until done, about one hour. When cool, remove meat from the bone and chop in bite-size pieces. Peel, then chop vegetables into small pieces; boil in a small amount of water about 10 minutes. They should be tender, but not completely done. Drain.

Make sauce by melting butter in a saucepan and adding flour until it is mixed. Gradually add milk, stirring constantly so the sauce will not lump. Add bouillon cubes, Worcestershire, salt, and pepper. Cook over low heat until mixture thickens. Mix chicken, vegetables, and sauce, and pour into a greased 3½-quart casserole. Top with biscuits rolled about ½ inch thick. (Any biscuit recipe will do, but a mix made according to directions will do as well.) Bake at 400° for 25–35 minutes until the casserole is bubbly and the biscuits are brown.

This may be frozen, but do not add the biscuits. If frozen, the cooking time will be longer, so the biscuits should be put on top the last 30 minutes of baking. Serves 4–6.

By Special Request (Louisiana)

Chicken "n" Dumplings

1 large hen, cut up
2 ribs celery and leaves, chopped
1 onion, chopped
1 sprig fresh thyme
1 bay leaf
1 carrot, sliced
1½ teaspoons salt
Pepper to taste
1 small green bell pepper, sliced

3 cups water
3 tablespoons butter or chicken fat
3 tablespoons all-purpose flour
¼ cup cream
1 (8-ounce) can mushrooms and
   liquid
½ cup green peas
1 (4-ounce) jar diced pimentos

Place chicken, celery, onion, thyme, bay leaf, carrot, salt, pepper, and green bell pepper with water in heavy covered pot, and cook until tender (about 2 hours). Remove from pot. Reserve stock after straining 3 times. Remove bones from hen, and cut meat into large pieces. Set aside. Heat butter in large pot. Add flour; blend until smooth and golden brown. Add chicken stock, cream, mushrooms, peas, pimentos, and chicken. Heat mixture until it reaches a low boil. Cover, and steam over low heat without lifting lid for 15 minutes.

DUMPLINGS:
2 cups all-purpose flour, sifted
1 tablespoon baking powder
½ tablespoon salt
¼ teaspoon red or white pepper
1 egg, well beaten

½ cup milk
1 tablespoon melted butter
¼ cup butter, softened
¼ cup chopped celery leaves
Chopped parsley for garnish

Sift flour, baking powder, salt, and pepper together. Combine beaten egg, milk, and melted butter. Add to dry ingredients. Stir just to moisten. Roll out ¼ inch thick. Spread with soft butter; sprinkle with celery leaves. Roll up, and slice into ½-inch slices. Place on top of hot chicken mixture. Cover, and steam on low heat without lifting lid for 15 minutes. Garnish with chopped parsley. Serves 6–8.

My Mother Cooked My Way Through Harvard with These Creole Recipes
(Mississippi)

Southern Pecan Chicken

Can substitute fish for the chicken for an equally good variation.

6–8 boneless chicken breasts	**½ cup finely chopped pecans**
Salt and pepper	**1 cup plain bread crumbs**
2 eggs	**¼ cup butter, divided**
2 teaspoons Creole mustard	**¼ cup vegetable oil, divided**

Lay chicken breasts out on wax paper. Season with salt and pepper. In a small bowl, beat eggs with mustard. In another bowl, combine pecans and bread crumbs. Dip chicken in egg mixture, then coat with bread crumb mixture.

Preheat oven to 350°. In a large skillet over medium-high heat, melt 2 tablespoons butter and 2 tablespoons oil. Sauté half the chicken until golden brown on each side. Place in an ovenproof dish. Wipe out skillet, pouring off any drippings (so second batch will have a clean, fresh look after browning). Sauté the rest of the chicken in the remaining 2 tablespoons of butter and oil. Place in oven, and bake for 15 minutes.

SAUCE:

¼ cup butter	**1 teaspoon lemon juice**
½ cup coarsely chopped pecans	

Melt butter in a small saucepan over low heat. Stir in pecans and lemon juice. Serve over chicken. Serves 6–8.

Kay Ewing's Cooking School Cookbook (Louisiana)

Mary Ann's Formal Yardbirds

This is an easy-to-prepare recipe because the chicken mix can be made a day ahead and refrigerated.

2 cups chopped cooked chicken
1 (3-ounce) package cream
   cheese, softened
2 tablespoons butter, softened
½ teaspoon salt
½ teaspoon pepper
2 tablespoons milk
1 tablespoon onion

1 tablespoon diced pimento
1 tablespoon Italian salad
   dressing
2 (8-ounce) packages crescent
   rolls
Melted butter
Crushed croutons
Paprika

Mix chicken, cream cheese, butter, salt, pepper, milk, onion, pimento, and salad dressing together; set aside. Press 2 crescent roll triangles at seam to form a rectangle; add ½ cup chicken mixture to center of each; pull up ends and twist. This can look like a giant candy kiss (or shape like birds). Brush with melted butter; sprinkle with crushed croutons and paprika. Bake at 350° for 20–25 minutes. Yields 8 servings.

Virginia Traditions (Virginia)

Champagne Chicken

2 tablespoons all-purpose flour
½ teaspoon salt
¼ teaspoon pepper
4 chicken breast halves, skinned
  and boned
2 tablespoons butter or margarine
1 tablespoon olive oil
¾ cup champagne or white wine
¾ cup sliced fresh mushrooms
½ cup whipping cream

Combine flour, salt, and pepper, and rub all over chicken. Heat butter and oil in large skillet. Add chicken, and brown about 5 minutes on each side. Add champagne, and cook over medium heat 15 minutes or until done. Remove chicken, and set aside. Add mushrooms and whipping cream to skillet. Cook over low heat, stirring constantly, until thick. Add chicken long enough to heat through. Serves 4.

Arkansas Favorites Cookbook (Arkansas)

Carolina Turkey Pie

A blue-ribbon winner in the North Carolina Turkey Association bake-off, this is a great recipe to use for leftover Thanksgiving turkey.

1 (10¾-ounce) can cream of
  celery soup
2 cups turkey broth
¾ cup self-rising cornmeal
1 cup self-rising flour
½ teaspoon poultry seasoning
½ teaspoon pepper
1 teaspoon dried sage
2 tablespoons chopped onion
1½ cups milk or buttermilk
½ cup margarine, melted
4 cups chopped cooked turkey

Bring the celery soup and broth to a boil in a saucepan. Combine cornmeal, self-rising flour, poultry seasoning, pepper, and sage in a bowl, and mix well. Stir in onion. Add milk and margarine, and mix well. Place turkey in a greased 9x13-inch baking dish. Pour broth mixture over turkey. Spread cornmeal mixture over top. Bake at 425° for 25 minutes or until brown. Yields 8 servings.

Seaboard to Sideboard (North Carolina)

Tony's Deep-Fried Turkey

The most requested recipe by far!

MARINADE:

1 tablespoon Worcestershire

2 tablespoons Creole mustard

3 (2-ounce) bottles garlic juice

3 (2-ounce) bottles onion juice

1 (3-ounce) bottle hot pepper
  sauce

¼ cup Tony's Creole Seasoning

8 ounces water

Mix the Marinade ingredients in a blender 2 days before cooking. Pour into a jar, and refrigerate. You can keep this in the refrigerator for months. Use at Thanksgiving then again at Christmas.

1 (approximately 14-pound)
  turkey (thawed, if frozen)

Creole mustard, to taste

Tony's Creole Seasoning, to taste

5 gallons peanut oil

Inject turkey with Marinade using a syringe. Rub turkey with additional mustard, and season generously with Tony's Creole Seasoning. When ready to cook, heat peanut oil to 350°; submerge turkey, and fry 4 minutes per pound of turkey. Yields 15 servings.

Tony Chachere's Second Helping (Louisiana)

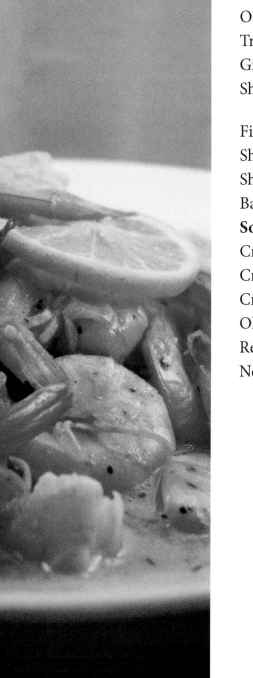

Onion Baked Catfish

**6 catfish fillets, each about
   6 ounces
½ teaspoon Creole seasoning
1 cup (8 ounces) sour cream
1 cup mayonnaise**

**1 (1-ounce) package ranch-style
   dry salad dressing mix
1 (6-ounce) can French fried
   onion rings**

Preheat oven to 350°. Put fillets in a shallow bowl, and sprinkle them evenly with Creole seasoning. Set aside. In a small bowl, combine sour cream, mayonnaise, and salad dressing mix. Blend well. Pour mixture into a shallow bowl.

Process onion rings in a blender or food processor until finely crushed. Put these in another shallow bowl. Dip fillets first in sour cream mixture, then in crushed onion rings, coating evenly. Put fish in an ungreased shallow baking pan. Bake uncovered until fish flakes easily when tested with a fork, about 20 minutes. Yields 6 servings.

Cajun Cooking for Beginners (Louisiana)

Traditional Southern-Fried Catfish

This catfish is served at fish fries and fish camps all over the South. Very easy.

Yellow or white cornmeal
Salt and pepper to taste
Catfish fillets or whole catfish,
** dressed**

Vegetable oil or shortening
Lemon wedges or tartar sauce
** (optional)**

Combine dry ingredients in a shallow bowl or pie pan. Rinse catfish under cool, running water, and pat dry with paper towels. For whole fish, cut 3 slits in each side before cooking. Dredge catfish in dry ingredients. Shake off excess.

Fill a heavy skillet half full of vegetable oil or shortening. When using a Dutch oven, add oil to a depth of at least 1½ inches. Heat oil to 375° over medium-high heat. Fry catfish in a single layer 2–4 minutes on each side, turning once, until fish is golden brown and flakes easily when tested with a fork. Cooking time will vary depending upon thickness of fish.

Drain fish on paper towels placed over a layer of newspaper or a brown paper bag. Serve with lemon wedges or tartar sauce, if desired.

The Essential Catfish Cookbook (Florida)

Grilled Marinated Grouper

⅓ cup lemon juice
1 teaspoon lemon rind
2 teaspoons prepared
   horseradish
½ garlic clove
½ teaspoon oregano
½ teaspoon basil

½ teaspoon salt
¼ teaspoon pepper
⅓ cup olive oil
8 (4-ounce) grouper fillets or other
   white fish
Vegetable cooking spray

In blender or food processor on low, combine lemon juice, lemon rind, horseradish, garlic, oregano, basil, salt, and pepper. Gradually add olive oil in a slow, steady stream. Set aside.

In a 9x13x2-inch baking dish, pour marinade over fish, turning to coat both sides. Cover, and refrigerate 8 hours or overnight.

Arrange fish in a fish grill basket coated with cooking spray. Grill, covered, over medium hot coals 7–8 minutes on each side, or until fish flakes easily when tested with a fork, basting frequently with marinade. Yields 8 servings.

Cookin' on Island Time (Florida)

Shrimp and Crab Stuffing for Flounder, Bass, Etc.

1 onion, minced
2 stalks celery, diced
¼ cup diced green bell pepper
4½ tablespoons butter
1 dozen shrimp, chopped
¼ cup fresh mushrooms
½ pound lump crabmeat

1 small bay leaf
Pinch of thyme
¼ pound almonds, browned,
   chopped fine
1 tablespoon Worcestershire
½ cup cream
3 ounces sherry

Sauté onion, celery, and bell pepper in butter till soft. Add shrimp and mushrooms; cover to produce liquid; uncover, and continue cooking till shrimp are barely pink. Add all other ingredients; stir and cook 5 minutes. Stuff fish, and bake at 375° until fish flakes easily when tested with a fork, about 10 minutes per pound. A greased sheet of brown paper under fish will keep it from sticking.

SAUCE FOR BASTING:

Blend a little butter, lemon juice, salt, Worcestershire, and Tabasco; add a little oil; pour over fish and baste often.

The Colonel's Inn Caterers'—Tallahassee Historical Cookbook (Florida)

Fish Seminole

4 fish fillets
¼ cup seasoned flour
2 eggs, beaten
Oil for sautéing
½ pound scallops
½ pound fresh mushrooms,
  sliced
¼ cup diced shallot
½ teaspoon salt
1 teaspoon chopped garlic
¼ teaspoon white pepper
Butter for sautéing
½ pound cooked crabmeat

Dredge fish in flour, then dip in egg. Sauté in a skillet in a small amount of oil until browned on both sides. Transfer to an oven, and bake at 450° until fish flakes easily with a fork, about 7–10 minutes.

To make topping, sauté scallops and next 5 ingredients together in a small amount of butter. Add crabmeat, and cook until hot. Spoon topping over cooked fish. Yields 4 servings.

Calypso Café (Florida)

Shrimp Creole

¾ cup chopped onion
3 cups thinly sliced celery
1 cup chopped green bell pepper
¼ cup margarine
1 (16-ounce) can tomatoes
3 tablespoons brown sugar
2 bay leaves
1½ teaspoons salt
¼ teaspoon pepper
3 tablespoons lemon juice
2 pounds shrimp (boiled in
  seasoned water); peeled

Sauté onion, celery, and bell pepper in margarine in skillet over low heat for 15 minutes. Add tomatoes, brown sugar, bay leaves, salt, and pepper; mix well. Simmer 30 minutes. Add lemon juice and shrimp. Simmer 6 minutes or until shrimp are heated through; discard bay leaves. Serve over rice. Yields 6 servings.

Calling All Cooks, Three (Alabama)

Shrimp Étouffée

ROUX:

6 tablespoons oil   **6 tablespoons all-purpose flour**

Heat oil over medium heat. When hot, add flour, and keep stirring until medium brown, about 20 minutes.

2 cups chopped onions	**1 teaspoon basil**
1 cup chopped bell pepper	**1 teaspoon chili powder**
1 cup chopped celery	**½ teaspoon cayenne**
5 garlic cloves, crushed	**¼ teaspoon black pepper**
1 small can stewed tomatoes	**1 teaspoon Season-All**
2 (10½-ounce) cans chicken broth	**3–4 pounds peeled shrimp**
2 cups water	**1 cup chopped green onions**
2 bay leaves	**2 tablespoons chopped parsley**

Add to Roux the onions, bell pepper, celery, and garlic; cook another 7 minutes. Add tomatoes, mixing well. Add chicken broth and water. While simmering, add spices. Let simmer 1 hour. Add shrimp, green onions, and parsley. Cook 20 minutes on very low heat, until shrimp is done. Serve over rice.

Nibbles Cooks Cajun (Arkansas)

Baked Stuffed Shrimp

Great company dish! Can be prepared earlier in the day and refrigerated. Large shrimp do just as well as jumbo.

24 raw jumbo shrimp, shelled, deveined
2 tablespoons plus 1 stick butter, divided
1 small onion, minced
¼ cup minced celery
½ green bell pepper, minced
1 tablespoon chopped parsley
1 pound backfin crabmeat
1 teaspoon salt
¼ teaspoon thyme
Dash of Tabasco
1 tablespoon Worcestershire
½ cup seasoned bread crumbs
1 egg, beaten
1 cup light cream or milk
1 stick butter
Paprika

Split shrimp lengthwise so they can be opened flat, but do not cut all the way through. Spread flat in buttered shallow baking dish, and set aside.

In 2 tablespoons butter, sauté onion, celery, and green pepper until onion is just transparent. Remove from heat. Add parsley. Toss vegetable mixture with crabmeat. Add seasonings, bread crumbs, egg, and cream. Toss gently. Mound crab mixture on shrimp. Melt stick of butter, and pour over shrimp. Sprinkle with paprika, and bake at 400° for 15 minutes. This can be prepared early in the day. If so, pour butter over shrimp just before baking. Yields 6 servings.

Food, Family, and Friendships (Virginia)

Soppin' Shrimp

¼ pound butter

⅔ cup lemon or lime juice

2½ teaspoons black pepper

1 teaspoon grated lemon rind

1½ cups Italian dressing

2 pounds raw shrimp, with shells

In medium saucepan, melt butter. Add juice, pepper, rind, and dressing, and bring to a boil. Add shrimp and simmer 6 minutes. Divide shrimp and sauce among 6 bowls. Serve with hot, crusty bread for soppin'. Yields 6 servings.

Historic Spanish Point: Cooking Then and Now (Florida)

Crawfish Pie

⅔ cup defatted chicken broth,
   less salt, divided
3 tablespoons diet margarine
1 large onion, chopped
½ green bell pepper, chopped
½ cup sliced celery
2 tablespoons all-purpose flour
1 pound crawfish tails, lightly
   rinsed and drained

6 ounces shredded low-fat
   mozzarella cheese (1½ cups)
½ cup plain bread crumbs
⅓ cup sliced green onions
¼ teaspoon salt
Pepper to taste
1 egg white
2 light pie crusts

In large skillet, heat ⅓ cup of broth and margarine. Sauté onion, bell pepper, and celery. Add flour; mix well. Add remaining ⅓ cup broth, and stir until well blended (this is a very thick mixture). Add crawfish tails, and stir over medium heat, about 5 minutes. Add cheese, bread crumbs, green onions, salt, and pepper. Mix well, and remove from heat.

Prepare pie crust. Place ½ crust mixture into a deep 9-inch pie plate. Place remaining crust (wrapped in plastic) in the refrigerator. Pour crawfish mixture into unbaked prepared pie shell. Roll out remaining crust between wax paper. Peel off one sheet of wax paper, place shell over pie, and remove the wax paper. Pinch edges together, trimming pie shell as needed. Cut several slits in pie shell, and brush with beaten egg white. Bake at 350° for 35 minutes. Yields 6 servings.

Per Serving: Cal 338; Fat 15.4g; %Fat Cal 41; Sat Fat 3.8g; Chol 90mg; Sod 353mg.

River Road Recipes III (Louisiana)

Crawfish Fettuccine

3 sticks butter
3 onions, chopped
2 green bell peppers, chopped
3 stalks celery, chopped
3 pounds crawfish tails
3 cloves garlic, minced

1 tablespoon chopped parsley
½ cup all-purpose flour
1 pint half-and-half
1 pound jalapeño cheese, cubed
12 ounces fettuccine

In a saucepan, melt butter and sauté onions, bell peppers, and celery until tender. Add crawfish, and simmer 10 minutes, stirring occasionally. Add garlic, parsley, flour, and half-and-half; mix well. Simmer on low heat for 30 minutes, stirring occasionally. Add cheese, and stir until melted. Meanwhile, cook noodles; drain, and cool. Combine noodles and sauce. Pour into a greased 6-quart casserole, or 2 greased 3-quart casseroles. Bake, uncovered, in a 300° oven for 20 minutes or until heated thoroughly. Freezes well. Serves 12.

Straight from the Galley Past & Present (Mississippi)

Crab Melt

1 pound crabmeat
¼ cup diced celery
¼ cup diced red onion
4 hard-boiled eggs, diced
½ teaspoon Old Bay Seasoning
¼ teaspoon dill weed

½ cup mayonnaise
¼ cup sour cream
4 English muffins
8 slices tomato
8 slices Cheddar cheese

Combine first 8 ingredients in a medium bowl. Separate muffins. Top each muffin half with 1 slice of tomato, crab mixture, and 1 slice of Cheddar. Broil in oven just until cheese melts. Serves 4.

The Main Street Mill Pub & Grill, Fort Royal
A Taste of Virginia History (Virginia)

Old Plantation Deviled Crab

2 tablespoons chopped onion
4 tablespoons butter, melted,
   divided
2 tablespoons all-purpose flour
¾ cup milk
½ teaspoon salt
Dash of pepper
½ teaspoon dry mustard
1 teaspoon Worcestershire
½ teaspoon sage
Dash of cayenne pepper
1 tablespoon lemon juice
1 egg, beaten
1 tablespoon chopped parsley
1 pound claw crabmeat
¼ cup dry bread crumbs

Cook onion in 3 tablespoons butter until tender. Blend in flour. Add milk gradually, and cook until thick, stirring constantly. Add seasonings and lemon juice. Stir a little of the sauce into the egg; add to remaining sauce, stirring constantly. Add parsley and crabmeat. Place in 6 well-greased (5-ounce) custard cups or individual crab shells. Place on baking pan or sheet. Combine remaining 1 tablespoon butter and crumbs; sprinkle over top of each shell. Bake at 350° for 15–20 minutes or until brown. Serves 6.

Crab Chatter (Georgia)

Rémoulade Sauce

½ cup tarragon vinegar
4 tablespoons Creole mustard
1 teaspoon horseradish
2 hard-boiled egg yolks, chopped
  fine
4 tablespoons mayonnaise
3 green onions and tops,
  chopped fine

1 large rib celery, chopped fine
3 teaspoons paprika
Dash of thyme
Dash of garlic salt
Dash of Worcestershire
Salt and cayenne pepper to taste
½ cup olive oil

In a bowl, whisk together all ingredients except salt, cayenne pepper, and olive oil. Whisk in olive oil a little at a time. Add salt and cayenne pepper to taste. Chill well.

If serving shrimp rémoulade, go ahead and add cooked, peeled shrimp before chilling.

Cooking on the Coast (Mississippi)

New Orleans Tartar Sauce

1 cup mayonnaise (freshly made
  with olive oil)
1 teaspoon powdered mustard
2 tablespoons minced parsley
½ clove garlic, put through
  press
1 teaspoon grated onion

⅛ teaspoon cayenne pepper
2 tablespoons chopped dill pickle
2 tablespoons capers, drained
  and chopped
1 tablespoon minced green
  onion tops

Combine all ingredients, mix well, and serve with fillet of trout or other seafood.

Louisiana's Original Creole Seafood Recipes (Louisiana)

Meats

Popover Mushroom Pizza Bake

BASE:

1 pound ground beef
1 pound fresh mushrooms, or
   1 (8-ounce) can mushrooms
½ cup chopped green bell
   pepper

½ cup chopped onion
1 (10½-ounce) can or jar pizza
   sauce with cheese
1 teaspoon oregano
1 teaspoon garlic salt

In large skillet or Dutch oven, cook and stir ground beef, mushrooms green pepper, and onion till meat is browned. Drain thoroughly. Stir in pizza sauce, oregano, and garlic salt. Simmer 10 minutes.

POPOVER TOPPING:

2 eggs
1 cup milk
1 tablespoon vegetable oil
1 cup all-purpose flour

Salt to taste
1½ cups shredded mozzarella
   cheese
½ cup grated Parmesan cheese

Preheat oven to 400°. In small bowl of electric mixer, blend together eggs, milk, and oil. Add flour and salt. Beat at medium speed about 1½ minutes, or till smooth. Spoon hot beef mixture into shallow 2-quart baking dish. Sprinkle with mozzarella cheese. Pour Popover Topping evenly over Base. Sprinkle with Parmesan cheese. Bake about 30 minutes, or till puffy and golden brown. Yields 6–8 servings.

Bethel Food Bazaar II (South Carolina)

Endless Meatloaf Sandwich

1 large loaf Italian bread,
   unsliced
½ teaspoon olive oil
1 pound lean ground beef or
   ground round
½ cup chopped green bell pepper
½ small onion, chopped

1 cup herbed bread crumbs
1 cup ketchup
1 package meatloaf seasoning
1 egg
2 splashes Worcestershire
1 dash salt

Cut top lengthwise from Italian bread. Set aside. Remove excess bread from loaf, making a cavity for the meatloaf mixture. Rub olive oil over cavity.

In a large bowl, mix ground beef, peppers, onion, bread crumbs, ketchup, seasoning, egg, Worcestershire, and salt. Place mixture in the bread cavity, and replace top of bread loaf. Cover with double sheets of foil to prevent bread from burning. Bake at 400° for 1 hour. Remove from oven; slice, and serve. Serves 4–6.

Bon Appétit: No Reservations Needed (Alabama)

Salisbury Steak and Gravy

1 pound ground beef
¾ teaspoon salt
½ teaspoon sage (optional)
1 tablespoon finely chopped
   onion
¼ cup cracker crumbs
¼ teaspoon pepper
1 egg
Oil for frying (2 tablespoons)

Combine ground beef, salt, sage, onion, crumbs, pepper, and egg. Mix well; form into 4 patties. Fry in lightly oiled frying pan until done and brown on both sides. Remove from skillet, and set aside.

GRAVY:
3 tablespoons all-purpose flour
2 cups hot water
2 beef bouillon cubes
Kitchen Bouquet (optional)

Stir flour in oil (3 tablespoons) left from frying patties. Stir in hot water in which bouillon has been dissolved. Stir and cook until thick. Put meat patties back in skillet with gravy, and simmer over low heat until heated through. Add a few drops of Kitchen Bouquet to brown gravy, if desired. Serves 4.

Not By Bread Alone Cookbook (Virginia)

Editor's Extra: Fry a little diced onion and garlic in pan before starting gravy for bolder flavor.

The Grierson Family's Upside Down Beef Pie

Benjamin Henry Grierson lead a group of 1,700 cavalry men known as Grierson's brigade in 1863. He was later promoted to the rank of major general.

1½ cups all-purpose flour
3 teaspoons baking powder
1 teaspoon salt, divided
1 teaspoon paprika
1 teaspoon celery salt
¼ teaspoon white pepper

5 tablespoons shortening, divided
¾ cup milk
¼ cup sliced onion
1 cup crushed tomatoes
¾ pound ground beef

In wooden mixing bowl, stir together flour, baking powder, ½ teaspoon salt, paprika, celery salt, and white pepper. Chop in with a fork 3 tablespoons shortening; mix thoroughly. Add milk; stir until well blended.

Melt remaining 2 tablespoons shortening in 9-inch cast-iron skillet. Add onions; fry until soft. Add tomatoes, remaining salt, and ground beef. Bring to boil. Take skillet off stove. Spread mixture from mixing bowl on top of meat mixture in skillet. Bake at 475° about 20 minutes. Turn out of skillet upside down on large plate or platter. Serves 8.

Civil War Period Cookery (Tennessee)

Oven BBQ Beef Brisket

3 tablespoons liquid smoke
1 (3- to 4-pound) boned beef
   brisket
Celery, onion, and garlic salts

Salt and pepper to taste
3 tablespoons Worcestershire
1 (6-ounce) bottle BBQ sauce

Pour liquid smoke over meat. Generously sprinkle both sides of brisket with celery, onion, and garlic salts. Cover, and refrigerate overnight.

Do not drain meat. Sprinkle with salt, pepper, and Worcestershire. Cover, and bake at 250° for 5 hours. Pour BBQ sauce over meat; bake uncovered 1 more hour with temperature raised to 350°. Serves 6–10.

Cooking with 257 (Florida)

Classic Slow-Cooked Ribs

Delicious prepared with either beef or pork ribs!

½–1 cup vinegar
½ cup ketchup
2 tablespoons sugar
2 tablespoons Worcestershire
1 clove garlic, minced
1 teaspoon dry mustard
1 teaspoon paprika

½ teaspoon salt
⅛ teaspoon pepper
2 pounds boneless pork or beef
   ribs, cut into serving-size
   pieces
1 tablespoon vegetable oil

Combine first 9 ingredients in slow cooker. Brown ribs in vegetable oil in a skillet. Transfer to slow cooker. Cover, and cook on LOW for 4–6 hours or until tender. Serves 4.

Dining Under the Carolina Moon (South Carolina)

Chicken Fried Steak

2 pounds tenderized round steak	**All-purpose flour** **½ cup vegetable oil**

Cut steak into 6–8 pieces. Flour each piece thoroughly and shake off excess. Dip in batter, flour again and shake off excess flour. Preheat oil, and cook meat 7–10 minutes until golden brown.

BATTER:

3 tablespoons sugar	**1 tablespoon baking powder**
½ teaspoon salt	**1½ cups milk, divided**
1 egg	

Mix first 4 ingredients with half the milk, and stir until smooth. Add remainder of milk, and mix well.

GRAVY:

¼ stick butter or margarine	**¼ cup all-purpose flour**
2 cups milk	**½ teaspoon salt**
⅛ cup vegetable cooking oil	**Pepper to taste**

Melt butter. Add milk and whisk thoroughly. Bring to a boil. Whisk flour into oil; add to heated milk. Stir until smooth and thickened. Remove from heat; add salt and pepper to taste. Serves 4–6.

A Great Taste of Arkansas (Arkansas)

Editor's Extra: Wipe most of the skillet out and make the gravy in a tad of the drippings. Delicious! Serve over rice alongside steaks.

Braised Sirloin Tips on Rice

2 tablespoons shortening
1½ pounds stew beef
1 (13-ounce) can beef consommé
⅓ cup plus ¼ cup water,
    divided

2 tablespoons soy sauce
¼ teaspoon onion salt
Dash of garlic salt
2 tablespoons cornstarch

Melt shortening in large skillet. Brown meat. Stir in consommé, ⅓ cup water, soy sauce, and salts. Heat to boiling. Reduce heat; cover, and simmer 1 hour or until meat is tender. Blend cornstarch and remaining ¼ cup water. Stir gradually into meat mixture. Cook, stirring constantly, until mixture boils. Boil and stir 1 minute. Serve over rice.

Koinonia Cooking (Tennessee)

Sunday Dinner Steaks

6–8 beef cubed steaks
¾ cup all-purpose flour
¾ teaspoon black pepper
Oil
1 envelope onion mushroom
    soup mix

1 (8-ounce) can mushrooms,
    undrained
1 medium onion, sliced thin
2 (10-ounce) cans beef gravy
2 cans water

Dredge steaks in flour/pepper mixture. Brown lightly on both sides in hot oil. Put steaks in 9x13-inch pan. Sprinkle with onion soup mix. Cover with mushrooms. Layer onion slices on top. Mix gravy and water together, and pour over steaks and onion. Do not stir. Cover tightly with foil. Bake at 250° for 3–4 hours. Serves 6–8.

Favorite Recipes: Bayside Baptist Church (Virginia)

Steak Creole with Cheese Grits

3 pounds lean, boneless
   top round steak
¼ teaspoon pepper
¼ cup all-purpose flour
1 onion, thickly sliced
2 green bell peppers, seeded
   and sliced
1 tablespoon minced garlic

2 cups canned beef broth
1 (15-ounce) can no-salt-added
   tomato sauce
1 teaspoon light brown sugar
1 tablespoon Worcestershire
1 teaspoon dried basil
1 teaspoon dried thyme
1 teaspoon dried oregano

Trim any fat from the round steak. Season with pepper and dredge in flour, shaking off any excess. In a large skillet coated with nonstick cooking spray, brown steak over medium-high heat for 5–7 minutes on each side. Remove steak, and set aside.

Add onion and pepper to skillet, and cook over moderate heat, stirring occasionally, about 5 minutes. Stir in garlic, beef broth, tomato sauce, brown sugar, Worcestershire, basil, thyme, and oregano, and bring to a boil. Return steak to the skillet, and spoon some of the sauce over it. Cover, and cook over medium-low heat for 1½–2 hours, or until the steak is very tender, stirring occasionally. Serve with Cheese Grits. Yields 6 servings.

CHEESE GRITS:

1 cup quick grits
3 cups water

1 cup shredded reduced-fat
   Cheddar cheese

Cook grits according to package directions, using 3 cups water and omitting any salt. When done, stir in Cheddar cheese.

Cal 487; Fat 10.4g; Cal from Fat 19.2%; Sat Fat 4.8g; Prot 61.7g; Carbo 32.9g; Sod 578g; Chol 143mg.

Trim & Terrific One-Dish Favorites (Louisiana)

Grilled Kentucky Bourbon Beef Tenderloin

1 (8-pound) beef tenderloin
2 garlic cloves, chopped
1 tablespoon freshly ground
   pepper
2 teaspoons Lawry's Seasoned
   Salt
1 cup vegetable oil
1 cup bourbon
¾ cup Worcestershire
2 tablespoons dry mustard
2 tablespoons chopped fresh
   parsley

Rub tenderloin with garlic, pepper, and seasoned salt. Place tenderloin in large shallow dish. Combine oil, bourbon, Worcestershire, dry mustard, and parsley in a bowl, and mix well. Pour oil mixture over tenderloin, turning to coat. Marinate, covered, in refrigerator 8 hours or longer, turning occasionally.

Arrange tenderloin on a grill rack. Sear over high heat; reduce heat to low. Grill 20–25 minutes for medium-rare, or to the desired degree of doneness. Let rest 10–15 minutes before slicing. Serves 15.

Note: Letting meat "rest" creates a juicier and more tender meat.

Home Again, Home Again (Kentucky)

Southern Shredded Pork

3½ pounds fresh pork

Place pork in a large pot and cover with water. Bring to a boil. Reduce to simmer, and cook until tender and easy to shred (approximately 1½ hours). Remove from water, and pull meat apart, discarding all fat.

SAUCE:

2 tablespoons margarine	**¼ cup water**
⅔ cup chopped onion	**3 tablespoons Worcestershire**
¼ cup vinegar	**1 teaspoon prepared mustard**
2 tablespoons brown sugar	**2 teaspoons salt**
1 cup ketchup	

In a saucepan, melt margarine. Add onion, and brown slightly. Add remaining Sauce ingredients, and simmer until blended. Add shredded pork, then simmer 15–20 minutes. Serve on buns or as a main course over rice. Serves 6–8.

Note: Beef may be used instead of pork. Substitute 3½ pounds stew beef and treat in same manner. Served in buns, this is a great item for a teen party.

Palm Beach Entertains (Florida)

Mandarin Pork Chops

4 (4-ounce) center-cut pork
   chops
1 tablespoon vegetable oil
½ cup orange juice
¼ cup water
3 tablespoons brown sugar
2 tablespoons lemon juice

1 tablespoon cornstarch
2 teaspoons chicken bouillon
   granules
1 (11-ounce) can Mandarin
   oranges, drained
1 medium green bell pepper,
   sliced

Brown pork chops on both sides in oil in a skillet. Remove from skillet, and set aside. Add orange juice, water, brown sugar, lemon juice, cornstarch, and bouillon to skillet. Cook until thickened, stirring constantly. Add pork chops. Simmer, covered, for 20 minutes or until pork chops are tender and cooked through. Add oranges and bell pepper. Cook until heated through. Yields 4 servings.

Calling All Cooks, Four (Alabama)

Stuffed Boned Pork Chops

6 (1-inch thick) pork chops or
   pork loin
1 egg
½ cup cornbread, crumbled
½ cup white bread, crumbled
⅓ cup chopped celery
¼ cup chopped onion
¼ cup chopped green bell pepper
   (optional)
1 tablespoon dry parsley (optional)
1 teaspoon salt
½ teaspoon pepper
¼ cup melted butter or pork stock
1 cup boiling water

Have pocket cut in pork chops on bone side. Beat egg, and add remaining ingredients, except boiling water. Stuff each chop or boned loin and hold together with toothpicks. Bake in 400° oven for 20 minutes, add boiling water, reduce heat to 300°, and bake 1 hour or until tender. Serves 6.

Florence Cook Book (Alabama)

Saucy Sausage

This is excellent served over rice as a main dish, or as a hearty appetizer.

2 pounds sausage (hot or mild)
1 cup sour cream
1 (9-ounce) bottle chutney, chopped
½ cup dry sherry

Shape sausage into small balls, and brown either in skillet, or in 350° oven about 20 minutes. (May be frozen at this point, if desired.)

   Mix sour cream, chutney, and sherry. Put in chafing dish. Add sausage balls. Serve with toothpicks. Yields 20 servings.

Note: Sausage links may be substituted for bulk sausage.

Dinner on the Diner (Tennessee)

Pork and Sausage Jambalaya

When the early Spanish settlers came to New Orleans in the early 1700s, they brought the recipes for their famous paella. Since many of the ingredients were not to be found in south Louisiana, their recipe was quickly adapted to the products at hand. Oysters and crawfish replaced clams and mussels in the recipe. Andouille took the place of ham, and the new dish emerged. Since the main ingredient was rice, the dish was named "Jambon a la yaya." Yaya is the African word for rice. Today, the dish is made with many variations and with whatever is available. The most popular combination, however, is pork, chicken, and andouille.—Chef John Folse

¼ cup shortening or bacon drippings	7 cups beef or chicken stock
2 pounds cubed pork	2 cups sliced mushrooms
1 pound andouille, sliced	1 cup sliced green onions
2 cups chopped onions	¼ cup chopped parsley
2 cups chopped celery	Salt and cayenne pepper to taste
1 cup chopped bell pepper	Dash of hot sauce
¼ cup diced garlic	4 cups long-grain rice

In a 2-gallon Dutch oven, heat shortening or bacon drippings over medium-high heat. Sauté cubed pork until dark brown on all sides and some pieces are sticking to bottom of pot, approximately 30 minutes. This is very important, as the brown color of jambalaya is derived from the color of the meat. Add andouille and stir-fry an additional 10–15 minutes. Tilt pot to one side and ladle out all oil, except for one large cooking spoon. Add onions, celery, bell pepper, and garlic. Continue cooking until all vegetables are well caramelized; however, be very careful, as vegetables will tend to scorch since the pot is so hot. Add stock, bring to a rolling boil, and reduce heat to a simmer. Cook all ingredients in stock approximately 15 minutes for flavors to develop. Add mushrooms, green onions, and parsley. Season to taste using salt, cayenne pepper, and hot sauce. I suggest that you slightly over-season since the rice tends to require a little extra seasoning. Add rice, cover, reduce heat to very low, and allow to cook 30–45 minutes, stirring at 15-minute intervals. Serves 8 or more.

The Evolution of Cajun & Creole Cuisine (Louisiana)

Cakes

Make and Wait Coconut Cake

The waiting is the secret to good taste; don't cheat and eat too soon!

1 (18¼-ounce) package
  butter-flavored cake mix
2 cups sugar
1 (8-ounce) carton sour cream

1 (12-ounce) package flaked
  coconut (if frozen, thawed)
1 (12-ounce) carton Cool Whip,
  thawed

Prepare cake according to directions, making 2 layers. Cool completely. Slice both layers horizontally making 4 thin layers. For frosting, combine sugar, sour cream, and coconut. Blend well, and chill. When chilled, reserve 1 cup frosting. Spread remaining frosting on top and side of each layer as you stack. Now add reserved 1 cup frosting to Cool Whip. Blend until smooth, and ice cake all over. Place in airtight container, and refrigerate 2 or 3 days. Serves 8–12.

Gran's Gems (Mississippi)

Company's Coming Coconut Cake

2 (6-ounce) packages frozen
   coconut
1 (8-ounce) carton sour cream
1½ cups sugar
1 (18¼-ounce) box yellow
   cake mix
1 (3-ounce) box vanilla instant
   pudding

½ cup cooking oil
1 cup water
1 teaspoon vanilla
2 eggs
2 egg yolks; save whites for
   Frosting

Combine coconut, sour cream, and sugar; set aside. In mixing bowl, combine remaining ingredients, and beat until smooth. Pour into 2 (9-inch) greased cake pans. Bake in 350° oven 30 minutes. Cool 10 minutes on rack. Split layers to make four. Spread coconut mixture between layers while warm. Frost cake. Serves 8–12.

COCONUT FROSTING:
2 reserved egg whites
¾ cup sugar
⅓ cup white Karo syrup
1 tablespoon water

¼ teaspoon cream of tartar
¼ teaspoon salt
¼ teaspoon vanilla
1 (3½-ounce) can flaked coconut

In double boiler, combine all ingredients except vanilla and coconut; cook 5 minutes, beating constantly at high speed. Remove from heat; add vanilla. Spread over cake; sprinkle with coconut.

When Dinnerbells Ring (Alabama)

Strawberry Pecan Cake

Elegant, beautiful, delicious.

1 (18¼-ounce) box white
   cake mix
1 (3-ounce) package strawberry
   Jell-O
1 cup Wesson oil

4 eggs
½ cup flaked coconut
1 cup frozen strawberries
1 cup chopped pecans

Mix in order given, and bake in 4 (8-inch) greased and floured cake pans at 350° about 25 minutes. Serves 8–12.

STRAWBERRY FROSTING:

1 stick margarine, softened
⅛ cup milk
½ cup frozen strawberries,
   drained

½ cup chopped pecans
1 (1-pound) box confectioners'
   sugar

Mix all ingredients together, gradually adding more milk or confectioners' sugar until desired consistency is reached. Frost cake when cooled.

Heart & Soul Cookbook (Alabama)

Editor's Extra: Okay to substitute 8–10 chopped fresh strawberries for frozen in frosting.

Red Velvet Cake

½ cup shortening
1½ cups sugar
2 eggs
1 (2-ounce) bottle red food
   coloring
2 tablespoons cocoa

1 tablespoon vanilla
1 cup buttermilk
2¼ cups cake flour
½ teaspoon salt
1 teaspoon baking soda
1 tablespoon vinegar

For batter, cream shortening and sugar. Add eggs. In 2-cup measuring cup, mix together red food coloring and cocoa to form a paste. Add to batter, then add vanilla. Sift flour and salt together; add alternately with buttermilk to batter. Beat well; fold in baking soda, then vinegar. Pour into 3 (10-inch) or 4 (8-inch) greased and floured cake pans. Bake at 300° for 20–30 minutes.

FROSTING:
2 tablespoons cornstarch
1 cup water
2 sticks butter, softened

1 cup sugar
1 teaspoon vanilla

Cook cornstarch and water on low heat; set aside to cool completely. Cream butter, sugar, and vanilla until thick. Add cornstarch mixture. Beat until like whipped topping. Spread between and on top of cooled layers. Serves 8–12.

Bountiful Blessings (South Carolina)

Toasted Butter Pecan Cake

3 tablespoons butter or
  margarine, melted
1⅓ cups chopped pecans,
  divided
¾ cup butter or margarine
  softened
1⅓ cups sugar
1½ teaspoons vanilla
2 eggs
2 cups sifted all-purpose flour
2 teaspoons baking powder
¼ teaspoon salt
⅔ cup milk

Toss melted butter and pecans. On a baking sheet, toast at 350° for 15 minutes, stirring occasionally.

Cream butter, and gradually add sugar; beat until light and fluffy. Add vanilla, and beat in eggs, one at a time. Sift together flour, baking powder, and salt; add dry ingredients to creamed mixture alternately with milk. Fold in 1 cup pecans. Pour batter into 2 (8-inch) greased and floured cake pans. Bake at 350° for 30–35 minutes. Cool slightly; remove from pans, and cool completely. Serves 8–12.

BUTTER PECAN FROSTING:

4 tablespoons butter or
  margarine, softened
3 cups sifted powdered sugar
2½–3 tablespoons light cream
1 teaspoon vanilla

Combine butter, sugar, cream, and vanilla; beat until smooth and creamy. Frost cake, and sprinkle remaining pecans on top.

A Taste of the Holidays (Georgia)

Peanut Butter Sheet Cake

1 cup water	1 teaspoon baking soda
½ cup oil	2 cups sugar
½ cup creamy peanut butter	2 eggs
½ cup butter	½ cup milk
2 cups all-purpose flour	1 teaspoon vanilla

Combine water, oil, peanut butter, and butter in large saucepan. Cook over medium heat, stirring constantly until smooth. Combine flour, baking soda, and sugar in a large bowl. Add eggs, milk, and vanilla. Beat at low speed until blended. Scrape peanut butter mixture into batter (but don't wash the pot, as you can make the frosting in it), and mix well. Pour batter into greased and floured 9x13-inch pan. Bake at 375° for 25 minutes. Cool.

PEANUT BUTTER FROSTING:

½ cup creamy peanut butter	4¾ cups sifted powdered sugar
½ cup butter	1 teaspoon vanilla
⅓ cup milk	

Combine peanut butter, butter, and milk in medium saucepan. Cook over medium heat, stirring constantly until smooth. Remove from heat. Add powdered sugar and vanilla. Stir until mixture is spreadable. Frost cake. Yields 15 servings.

Linen Napkins to Paper Plates (Tennessee)

Editor's Extra: Fun to decorate with chocolate chips or mini M&Ms. Makes a lovely layer cake, too.

Key Lime Cake

1 (18¼-ounce) package Duncan
   Hines Lemon Supreme
   Cake Mix
½ cup water

½ cup Key lime juice
1 (3-ounce) package lime gelatin
½ cup vegetable oil
4 eggs

With electric mixer, blend all ingredients together on medium speed about 2 minutes. Pour into a greased 9x13-inch baking pan, and bake at 325° for 35–45 minutes till toothpick in center comes out nearly clean. After removing from oven, use an ice pick and prick through cake, top to bottom, many times. Drizzle with icing while cake is still warm. Add whipped topping, if desired. Serves 8–12.

KEY LIME ICING:
2 cups powdered sugar   ¼ cup Key lime juice

Mix powdered sugar and lime juice.

Country Club Cooks (Florida)

Editor's Extra: This can also be baked in a greased tube or Bundt pan for 7–10 minutes longer. If Key limes are not available, do not hesitate to use regular limes. Moist and delicious.

Earthquake Cake

TOPPING:

2 cups powdered sugar
2 (3-ounce) packages cream
   cheese, softened

1 teaspoon vanilla

Cream sugar, cream cheese, and vanilla; set aside.

CAKE:

1 cup flaked coconut
1 cup chopped pecans

1 (18¼-ounce) package German
   chocolate cake mix

Preheat oven to 350°. Grease and flour a 9x13-inch baking dish. Combine coconut and pecans. Spread in bottom of dish. Prepare cake mix according to package directions. Pour batter over coconut and nut layer; do not stir.

Drop Topping mixture by spoonfuls over cake, without coming in contact with sides of dish. Do not stir. Bake 55 minutes or until toothpick or cake tester comes out clean. Cool in pan 5 minutes. Run a knife around edges, and invert onto a serving plate. May be served plain or with whipped cream or ice cream. Yields 10–12 servings.

Catering to Charleston (South Carolina)

Southern Fudge Cake

CAKE:

2 cups sugar
2 cups all-purpose flour
1 teaspoon baking soda
1 cup margarine or butter
4 tablespoons cocoa

1 cup water
½ cup buttermilk
1 teaspoon vanilla
2 eggs, beaten

Mix sugar, flour, and baking soda in large bowl; set aside. Combine butter, cocoa, and water in saucepan; bring almost to a boil, but do not boil. Pour over sugar mixture, and mix well. Add buttermilk, vanilla, and eggs, and mix well. Pour into greased 9x13-inch baking pan. Bake at 400° for 20–25 minutes.

ICING:

½ cup margarine or butter
4 tablespoons cocoa
⅓ cup milk
1 teaspoon vanilla

1 (16-ounce) box powdered
   sugar
1 cup chopped nuts

Combine butter, cocoa, and milk in saucepan. Bring almost to a boil, but do not boil. Stir in vanilla, sugar, and nuts, and spread on cake while hot.

Gracious Goodness . . . Charleston! (South Carolina)

Chocolate Cream Supreme

1 (18¼-ounce) package dark
   chocolate cake mix
1 (1¼-ounce) envelope whipped
   topping mix (Dream Whip)
1 (4-ounce) package vanilla
   instant pudding mix

1½ cups cold milk
1 (16-ounce) can creamy milk
   chocolate frosting
1 (12-ounce) container frozen
   whipped topping, thawed

Prepare and bake cake as directed on package in 2 (8-inch) greased and floured cake pans. Cool, and split layers to make 4. Blend topping mix, pudding mix, and cold milk; beat until stiff. Spread ½ this Filling on bottom layer of cake (remaining, later, on third layer). Make Glaze for top of cake by heating ⅔ cup frosting slightly. For second layer, make Chocolate Cream by folding remaining frosting into thawed whipped topping; ⅓ goes on second layer, and remainder around sides of cake after glazing top. Spectacular! Keep cake refrigerated (if there's any left).

Bountiful Blessings from the Bauknight Table (South Carolina)

Darn Good Chocolate Cake

1 (18¼-ounce) package devil's
  food chocolate cake mix
1 (3½-ounce) package
  chocolate instant pudding
1¾ cups sour cream

¾ cup vegetable oil
½ cup warm water
4 eggs
1½ cups milk chocolate chips

Mix together cake mix and pudding mix. Add sour cream, vegetable oil, water, and eggs; mix well. Stir in chocolate chips. Spray Bundt pan with cooking spray; pour in batter, and bake at 350° for 50–60 minutes, until firm to touch, or when toothpick comes out clean.

Heaven in a Pot (Florida)

Apple Dapple Cake with Glaze

2 cups sugar
1¼ cups Crisco oil
4 eggs
1 teaspoon vanilla

3 cups self-rising flour
½ teaspoon cinnamon
1 cup chopped nuts
3 cups chopped raw apples

Beat sugar, oil, and eggs well. Add vanilla, flour, and cinnamon; beat well. Stir in nuts and apples, mixing thoroughly by hand. Pour into greased and floured tube pan. Bake 1 hour 15 minutes at 350°. Cool 30 minutes; turn onto cake plate. Poke holes in top with toothpick; add Glaze.

GLAZE:
1 cup light brown sugar
1 stick butter

¼ cup milk
Dash of cinnamon

Mix all ingredients in a saucepan, and bring to a boil over medium heat. Cook one minute. Pour over warm cake, allowing Glaze to run down sides and into center. Serves 8–10.

Pleasant Grove Baptist Church Cookbook (Alabama)

Apricot Brandy Pound Cake

1 cup butter or margarine, softened
3 cups sugar
6 eggs
3 cups all-purpose flour
¼ teaspoon baking soda
¼ teaspoon salt

1 (8-ounce) carton sour cream
½ cup apricot brandy
1 teaspoon orange extract
1 teaspoon vanilla extract
½ teaspoon lemon extract
½ teaspoon rum extract
¼ teaspoon almond extract

Cream softened butter; gradually add sugar, beating until mixture is light and fluffy. Add eggs, one at a time, beating well after each addition. Combine flour, baking soda, and salt, and set aside. Combine sour cream, brandy, and flavorings. Add to creamed mixture alternately with flour mixture; beginning and ending with flour mixture. Pour batter into a greased and floured 10-inch tube pan. Bake 325° for 1 hour 20 minutes, or until wooden toothpick inserted in center comes out clean. Cool in pan 10–15 minutes. Remove from pan, and cool completely. Serves 10–16.

Mountain Laurel Encore (Kentucky)

Editor's Extra: Pretty with a powdered sugar glaze.

Million Dollar Pound Cake

This is the best pound cake I've ever eaten, but it is a large cake and needs a large mixing bowl and a heavy-duty beater.

6 eggs	¼ teaspoon salt
1 pound butter or margarine	1 teaspoon almond extract
1 cup milk	4 cups all-purpose flour
3 cups sugar	

Have eggs, butter, and milk at room temperature. Cream butter, sugar, and salt well. Add almond extract. Add eggs one at a time, beating really well. Add flour and milk a little at a time, and beat well until batter is smooth. Grease a 10-inch tube pan well, and dust with flour. Bake in a preheated 325° oven for 1 hour 40 minutes. Test for doneness with a toothpick; when it comes out clean, the cake is done.

CARAMEL ICING:

2 cups brown sugar	6 tablespoons butter
½ cup half-and-half	

Cook all ingredients slowly in a heavy pan until it forms a soft ball when tested in water. Remove from heat, and beat by hand until it starts creaming. This is a long, tiring process, but well worth the effort. If icing hardens before you are finished, you may add a little more half-and-half or milk to keep it spreadable. Serves 15–20.

The Best of the Bushel (Virginia)

Editor's Extra: To effectively grease Bundt pans, brush generously with melted shorteneing.

"Island" Rum Cake

Irresistibly good!

1 cup chopped nuts, reserve
   ¼ cup
1 (18¼-ounce) package yellow
   cake mix
4 eggs, beaten

1 (3-ounce) package vanilla
   instant pudding mix
½ cup vegetable oil
½ cup water
½ cup rum

Grease and flour a Bundt cake pan. Sprinkle with reserved nut meats. Combine remaining ingredients; mix well, and pour into pan. Bake at 325° for 50–60 minutes. Prepare Glaze.

GLAZE:

¼ cup rum
¼ cup water

½ cup margarine
1 cup sugar

Combine ingredients in a saucepan; boil 2 minutes. Pour over hot cake while still in the pan, pulling cake away from sides of pan; cool ½ hour before removing from pan.

'Pon Top Edisto (South Carolina)

Editor's Extra: To effectively grease Bundt pans, brush generously with melted shorteneing.

Almond Torte with Raspberry Sauce

RASPBERRY SAUCE:

1 (16-ounce) package frozen
   raspberries, thawed and
   drained

½ cup sugar

Mix raspberries and sugar in a bowl. Chill, covered, in the refrigerator.

TORTE AND ASSEMBLY:

7 ounces almond paste
¾ cup sugar
½ cup (1 stick) butter,
   softened
3 eggs
½ cup all-purpose flour, sifted

⅓ teaspoon baking powder
1 tablespoon amaretto
¼ teaspoon vanilla extract
Confectioners' sugar
Fresh raspberries for garnish

Combine almond paste, sugar, and butter in a mixing bowl, and beat until blended. Add eggs one at a time, mixing well after each addition. Stir in mixture of flour and baking powder. Add amaretto and vanilla, and mix well; do not overbeat. Spread in greased 8-inch baking dish. Bake at 350° for 40–50 minutes or until edge pulls from side of dish. Cool in pan, and cut into 8 wedges. Serve with Raspberry Sauce and confectioners' sugar. Garnish with fresh raspberries. Serves 8.

Note: Soften almond paste by placing in a resealable plastic bag with sliced apples or a couple of slices of fresh bread for 8–10 hours.

Home Again, Home Again (Kentucky)

White Chocolate and Lime Mousse Cake

This is so good and light . . . a refreshing cloud in your mouth.

CRUST:

2 cups ground gingersnap
   cookies (about 38 cookies)

2 tablespoons sugar

5 tablespoons unsalted butter,
   melted

Combine cookie crumbs and sugar in food processor. Add butter, and pulse until moist clumps form. Press mixture into bottom and 1 inch up sides of a 10-inch springform pan.

FILLING:

½ cup Key lime juice

1 (¼-ounce) envelope
   unflavored gelatin

½ cup heavy cream

9 ounces white chocolate,
   chopped

1 (8-ounce) package cream
   cheese, softened

2 (8-ounce) packages reduced-fat
   cream cheese, softened

1 cup sugar

3 tablespoons lime zest

2 cups heavy cream, chilled and
   whipped

Place lime juice in a glass bowl. Sprinkle gelatin over top to soften. Bring cream to a simmer in a heavy medium-size saucepan. Remove from heat, and add white chocolate. Stir until melted and smooth. Stir in gelatin mixture. Cool slightly.

In a large bowl, beat cream cheese, sugar, and lime zest with an electric mixer until blended. Slowly beat in white chocolate mixture. Fold in whipped cream. Pour Filling over Crust in pan. Cover, and refrigerate overnight or up to 2 days. Release sides of pan from cake. Transfer to a cake platter, and serve. Yields 12–14 servings.

Key Ingredients (Tennessee)

Toffee Cheesecake Temptations

Creamy and rich bite-size cheesecakes. Ideal to serve on a buffet.

⅔ cup butter or margarine,
softened
¾ cup packed brown sugar
2 cups all-purpose flour
½ cup chopped pecans
16 ounces cream cheese,
softened

¾ cup sugar
2 large eggs
1 tablespoon lemon juice
2 teaspoons vanilla extract
1 (7-ounce) Heath Bar, crushed

Beat butter at medium speed in mixing bowl until light. Add brown sugar gradually, beating until fluffy. Add flour, and mix well. Stir in pecans. Set aside 1 cup mixture. Press remaining mixture over bottom of a greased 9x13-inch baking pan. Bake at 350° for 14–15 minutes or until light brown.

Beat cream cheese at medium speed in mixing bowl until smooth. Add sugar gradually, beating until light and fluffy. Beat in eggs one at a time. Stir in lemon juice and vanilla. Pour over hot crust. Sprinkle reserved crumb mixture evenly over batter. Bake at 350° for 25 minutes or until nearly set; cheesecake will firm when chilled. Sprinkle candy over hot cheesecake. Cool on a wire rack. Chill, covered, for 8 hours. Cut into bars to serve. Yields 3 dozen.

Savor the Moment (Florida)

Company Pecan Cheesecake

This is a very special Christmas dessert. Top with a sprig of holly. It will serve a crowd.

1 cup graham cracker crumbs
3 tablespoons sugar
3 tablespoons butter, melted
½ cup finely chopped pecans
3 (8-ounce) packages cream
  cheese, softened
1¼ cups firmly packed dark
  brown sugar

2 tablespoons all-purpose flour
3 eggs
1½ teaspoons vanilla
¾ cup chopped pecans
Maple syrup
Pecan halves

Combine crumbs, sugar, butter, and pecans. Press into the bottom of a 9-inch springform pan. Bake at 350° for 10 minutes. Set aside to cool.

Combine cream cheese, sugar, and flour; mix well. Add eggs, one at a time, beating after each addition. Blend in vanilla and chopped pecans. Pour into crust, and bake at 350° for 50–55 minutes. Cool. Remove from pan. Chill. Brush with syrup, and garnish with pecan halves. Yields 1 (9-inch) cheesecake.

Taste Buds (North Carolina)

Dianne's Cherry Cheesecake

This tastes even better than it looks, and it's gorgeous.

CRUST:

1½ cups graham cracker
   crumbs
3 tablespoons sugar
¼ teaspoon cinnamon
4 tablespoons melted butter

Combine Crust ingredients, and press in a well-buttered 9-inch spring-form pan. Bake at 350° for 10 minutes.

FILLING:

3 (8-ounce) packages cream
   cheese, softened
2 teaspoons lemon juice
1 cup plus 2 tablespoons sugar,
   divided
¼ teaspoon salt
5 large eggs
1½ cups dairy sour cream
½ teaspoon vanilla
1 (21-ounce) can cherry pie filling,
   chilled

Preheat oven to 350°. Beat softened cream cheese with electric beater till creamy; add lemon juice, and beat till smooth. Add 1 cup sugar, salt, and eggs, all at one time. Beat at medium speed until well blended. Then beat for 10 minutes more until mixture is smooth and lemon-colored. Pour into prepared pan, and bake 45 minutes.

Remove from oven (leave oven on), and let cake stand 20 minutes. With a spoon, stir sour cream, remaining 2 tablespoons sugar, and vanilla together until sugar is dissolved. Spread on cake, and return to oven 10 more minutes. Cool. Chill. Spread chilled pie filling on top.

Granny's Taste of Christmas (North Carolina)

Cookies & Candies

Peanut Butter Cookies

⅔ cup all-purpose flour
1 teaspoon baking powder
¼ teaspoon salt
½ cup chunky peanut butter

¼ cup margarine, softened
1 cup packed brown sugar
1 teaspoon vanilla extract
2 eggs

Sift flour, baking powder, and salt together. Cream peanut butter and margarine in mixer bowl until light and fluffy. Add brown sugar and vanilla; beat well. Beat in eggs. Add dry ingredients; beat well. Spread in greased 8x8-inch baking pan. Bake at 350° for 25–30 minutes or until top looks dry and wooden pick inserted in center comes out clean. Cool in pan on wire rack. Cut into 2-inch squares. Yields 16 servings.

From Our House to Yours (Georgia)

Editor's Extra: Or make drop cookies—about 12 minutes at 375°.

Five Cup Cookies

An established favorite.

1 stick butter
1 cup graham cracker crumbs
1 cup chocolate chips
1 cup peanut butter chips

1 cup flaked coconut
1 cup chopped pecans
1 (14-ounce) can Eagle Brand
  sweetened condensed milk

Preheat oven to 325°. Place butter in 8½x11-inch pan in oven until butter is melted. Remove from oven, and spread graham cracker crumbs all over bottom of pan. Spread chocolate chips, peanut butter chips, coconut, and chopped pecans, in that order, over graham cracker crumbs. Pour whole can of Eagle Brand milk on top of all ingredients. Bake at 325° for 10–15 minutes or until golden brown. Let cool for 30 minutes, then cut into squares. Yields 24–30 cookies.

Somethin's Cookin' at LG&E (Kentucky)

Southern Sand Tarts

2 cups all-purpose flour, sifted
1 (1-pound) box powdered sugar,
  divided

2 sticks margarine, softened
1 tablespoon vanilla
1½ cups chopped pecans

Sift together flour and 7 tablespoons powdered sugar; blend flour and sugar with margarine. Add vanilla, and mix well; add chopped pecans, and mix well. Place in covered bowl, and refrigerate overnight or longer.

Roll chilled dough into neat balls (or ovals, or crescents). Place on lightly greased cookie sheet, and bake at 325° for 20–25 minutes, till slightly brown. (Do not overcook.)

Remove from oven. Leave on cookie sheet 7–10 minutes. Then gently roll all cookies at once in remainder of powdered sugar that has been sifted into a heavy paper bag. Cookies will absorb most all the sugar. Pour into container that can be sealed. Yields 110–118 cookies.

Down Here Men Don't Cook (Mississippi)

English Toffee Cookies

½ cup butter
½ cup margarine
1 cup sugar
1 egg yolk
1 teaspoon vanilla

2 cups all-purpose flour
½ teaspoon salt
1 egg white, beaten
2 cups chopped pecans

Blend butter, margarine, and sugar in food processor or electric mixer until creamy. Add egg yolk and vanilla, and blend. Add flour and salt, and blend. Let dough stand in refrigerator at least 30 minutes. With the palm of your hand, spread very thin on cookie sheet, covering it completely. Lightly brush with beaten egg white. Sprinkle with chopped pecans. Bake at 375° for 12–15 minutes or until light brown. Let cool about 5 minutes, and cut into small rectangles. Yields 3 dozen.

Feasts of Eden (Arkansas)

Pecan Cookies

1½ cups butter or margarine,
  melted
1 cup white sugar
1 cup light brown sugar
3 eggs
2 teaspoons vanilla

5 cups all-purpose flour
1 teaspoon baking soda
1 teaspoon nutmeg
¼ teaspoon salt
6 cups chopped pecans

Combine butter, sugars, and eggs in mixer bowl. Beat well, and add vanilla, flour, baking soda, nutmeg, salt, and pecans. When this is well mixed, chill in refrigerator. Divide dough into 4 parts. Work each one forming a roll; these are long rolls. Wrap in plastic wrap, and freeze. When you get ready to bake, slice really thin; put on a sprayed cookie sheet. Bake at 250° for 25 minutes. Remove from cookie sheet quickly. Cool, and store in an air tight container. Yields over 100 cookies.

Gibson/Goree Family Favorites (Alabama)

Toffee Pecan Bites

A crispy, tasty, gem of a cookie.

Graham crackers (about 24 squares)
2 sticks margarine

1 cup light brown sugar
1 cup finely chopped pecans

Fill large cookie sheet with crackers laid with sides touching. (Don't break crackers while placing in pan, because this will cause the syrup to run down in the pan and off the cookie.) Bring margarine and brown sugar to a boil. Boil for 5 minutes, stirring constantly. Remove from heat. Add chopped pecans. Pour this mixture over graham crackers that have been placed flat on a large cookie sheet. Bake at 325° for exactly 10 minutes. When completely cool, break into bites.

Mississippi Stars Cookbook (Mississippi)

Crunchy Key Lime Cookies

Mouth-watering cookies with a tropical flair, made with the juice and rind of the Key lime—a small yellow lime native to Florida.

½ cup (1 stick) butter or
   margarine, softened
1½ cups confectioners' sugar
1 egg
1 tablespoon Key lime juice

2 teaspoons grated Key lime zest
1 cup all-purpose flour
1 teaspoon baking powder
¼ teaspoon salt
2 cups cornflakes, crushed

Cream butter and confectioners' sugar in a mixing bowl until light and fluffy. Stir in egg, Key lime juice, and zest (mixture may appear curdled). Add flour, baking powder, and salt, and mix well.

Drop dough by teaspoonfuls into cornflakes, and turn to coat. Place on ungreased cookie sheets. Bake at 350° for 12–16 minutes. Remove to a wire rack to cool. Yields 2 dozen.

Savor the Moment (Florida)

Cornflake Crinkles

1 cup butter, softened
1 cup sugar
1½ cups sifted all-purpose flour
1 teaspoon cream of tartar
½ teaspoon salt

1 teaspoon baking soda
1 teaspoon vanilla
4 cups cornflakes cereal
1 cup chopped pecans

Combine butter and sugar. Beat until smooth and creamy. Combine flour, cream of tartar, salt, and baking soda; gradually add to butter mixture. Add vanilla; beat until smooth and well blended. Gently fold in cornflakes and pecans so as not to crush cereal. Drop by teaspoonfuls onto ungreased cookie sheet. Bake at 300° for 12–15 minutes or until lightly browned. Yields about 3½ dozen.

Holiday Delights (Georgia)

Nannie White's Potato Chip Crunch Cookies

Delicious and crunchy. A dainty party cookie.

1 cup butter or margarine,
  softened
½ cup sugar
1 teaspoon vanilla

1½ cups crushed potato chips
½ cup chopped pecans
2 cups sifted all-purpose flour

Cream together butter or margarine, sugar, and vanilla. Add crushed potato chips and chopped pecans. Sift in flour. Form into small balls, using about 1 teaspoon dough for each. Place on ungreased cookie sheet. Press balls flat with bottom of a tumbler dipped in sugar. Bake at 350° for 16–18 minutes, or until cookies are lightly browned. If desired, sprinkle with colored sugar crystals, and top each cookie with pecan half or candied cherry half. Yields 3½ dozen cookies.

Granny's Kitchen (Virginia)

Benne Seed Wafers

¾ cup butter or margarine,
   softened
2 cups brown sugar
1 egg, beaten
1 cup all-purpose flour

¼ teaspoon salt
½ teaspoon baking powder
1 teaspoon vanilla
¾ cup toasted benne seeds
   (sesame)

Cream butter and sugar; add beaten egg, then flour sifted with salt and baking powder. Add vanilla and benne seeds. Drop by teaspoonfuls (or less) onto greased cookie sheet. Bake in 325° oven 8–10 minutes. Allow to cool 1 minute before removing from pan. This makes a transparent wafer. Yields about 100.

Charleston Receipts (South Carolina)

Chocolate-Filled Snowballs

1 cup butter, softened
½ cup sugar
1 teaspoon vanilla
2 cups all-purpose flour, sifted

1 cup finely chopped pecans
1 (5¾-ounce) package chocolate
   kisses, unwrapped
Confectioners' sugar

Cream butter, sugar, and vanilla till very light and fluffy. Add sifted flour and pecans, blending well. Cover bowl with plastic wrap, and chill dough about 1 hour. Remove foil wrappers from kisses.

Preheat oven to 375°. Shape dough around kisses, using about 1 tablespoon of dough for each. Cover kiss completely. Bake 12 minutes till set, not brown. Remove from cookie sheet onto absorbent paper, and cool slightly. While still warm, roll in confectioners' sugar. Cool completely before storing. Roll in confectioners' again, if desired. Yields 5 dozen.

Bravo (North Carolina)

Chocolate Chubbies

6 ounces semisweet chocolate, cut into small pieces
2 ounces unsweetened chocolate, cut into small pieces
5 tablespoons unsalted butter
3 eggs
1 cup (scant) sugar
¼ cup all-purpose flour
½ teaspoon (scant) baking powder
Pinch of salt
8 ounces semisweet chocolate chips
8 ounces broken-up pecans
8 ounces broken-up walnuts

Combine semisweet and unsweetened chocolate pieces with butter in top of a double boiler. Cook over hot water until chocolate is melted, stirring frequently. Remove from heat, and let stand to cool slightly. Beat eggs and sugar in a bowl until smooth. Add cooled chocolate mixture, beating constantly.

Sift flour, baking powder, and salt together into a bowl. Add to the chocolate mixture, stirring until moistened. Fold in chocolate chips, pecans, and walnuts. Drop batter by tablespoonfuls onto 2 greased cookie sheets, leaving 2 inches between cookies. Bake at 325° for 15–20 minutes or until lightly browned. Yields 3 dozen large cookies.

Southern Scrumptious: How to Cater Your Own Party (Alabama)

Sour Cream Cookies

2¼ cups all-purpose flour
1½ teaspoons baking powder
½ teaspoon baking soda
½ teaspoon salt
¼ teaspoon allspice
¼ teaspoon nutmeg
½ cup chopped nuts (more,
   if desired)

½ cup butter or margarine,
   softened
⅔ cup firmly packed light brown
   sugar
1 egg, unbeaten
¼ cup sour cream
½ cup raisins

Sift all dry ingredients together. Cream butter and brown sugar; add egg, and beat well. Add dry ingredients, alternately with sour cream. Stir in raisins. Drop cookies onto greased cookie sheet; bake at 375° for 10–12 minutes.

Smoky Mountain Magic (Tennessee)

Pecan Squares

CRUST:
3 cups all-purpose flour
½ cup sugar
½ teaspoon salt

1 cup butter or margarine,
   softened

In large mixing bowl, blend together flour, sugar, salt, and margarine until mixture resembles coarse crumbs. Press firmly and evenly into a greased, 10x15x1-inch baking dish. Bake at 350° for 20 minutes.

FILLING:
4 eggs
1½ cups light or dark corn syrup
1½ cups sugar

3 tablespoons margarine, melted
1½ teaspoons vanilla
2½ cups chopped pecans

In a bowl, combine all ingredients, except pecans. Spread evenly over hot Crust. Sprinkle pecans evenly over top. Bake at 350° for 25 minutes or until set. Cool on a wire rack. Yields 4 dozen squares.

Down Home Dining in Mississippi (Mississippi)

Chocolate Mint Squares

CAKE LAYER:

½ cup butter, softened
1 cup sugar
2 eggs
½ cup all-purpose flour

2 (1-ounce) squares unsweetened
   chocolate, melted
½ cup chopped pecans

Cream butter and sugar until light and fluffy. Add eggs, and beat thoroughly. Add flour, and blend well. Add chocolate, blending thoroughly; stir in pecans. Pour into greased 9x9-inch pan. Bake at 350° for 20 minutes. Cool in pan.

PEPPERMINT FILLING:

1 tablespoon butter, softened
1 cup confectioners' sugar

2 tablespoons crème de menthe

Blend butter and sugar. Stir in crème de menthe until of spreading consistency. Spread over Cake Layer. Chill. (Okay to double sugar and butter for thicker filling.)

CHOCOLATE GLAZE:

2 (1-ounce) squares semisweet
   chocolate

1 tablespoon butter

Melt chocolate and butter, stirring well. Spread on cold Peppermint Filling. Chill; cut into 1-inch squares. Store in refrigerator. Yields 4 dozen.

Heart of the Palms (Florida)

Carmelitas

32 caramels, unwrapped
5 tablespoons cream
1 cup all-purpose flour
1 cup quick oatmeal
¾ cup packed brown sugar
½ teaspoon baking soda
¼ teaspoon salt
¾ cup butter, melted
1 (8-ounce) package semisweet
  chocolate chips
½ cup chopped pecans

Preheat oven to 350°. Melt caramels and cream in double boiler. Set aside. Combine flour, oatmeal, sugar, soda, salt, and butter. Press half of crumbs into a 9x13-inch pan. Bake at 350° for 10 minutes.

Spread caramel mixture over crust, then chips and pecans. Sprinkle with remaining crumb mixture. Bake another 15–20 minutes. Chill one hour. Cut into bars. Yields 24.

Tidewater on the Half Shell (Virginia)

Chewy Caramel Brownies

These indulgent brownies will be the talk of the town. These brownies harden as they cool and become easier to cut, so try to wait—I never can!

9 ounces caramels, unwrapped
1 (14-ounce) can low-fat
**   sweetened condensed milk,**
**   divided**
1 (18¼-ounce) box reduced-fat
**   devil's food cake mix**

½ cup (1 stick) light margarine,
**   melted**
½ cup semisweet chocolate chips

Preheat the oven to 350°. Coat a 9x13x2-inch baking pan with non-stick cooking spray, and dust with flour. In the top of a double boiler or in the microwave, melt the caramels with ⅓ cup condensed milk. Keep warm, and set aside. In a large mixing bowl, combine the cake mix, margarine, and remaining condensed milk. Beat at high speed with a mixer until very well combined.

Spread half of the dough into the bottom of the baking pan. Bake for 6 minutes, then sprinkle chocolate chips over the partially baked dough. Spread caramel mixture over chocolate chips. Crumble remaining dough on top. Return to oven, and continue baking for 15 minutes, or until the sides pull away from the pan. Do not overcook. Cool in the pan on a rack, and cut into squares. Yields 48 brownies.

Cal 116; Fat 2.9g; Cal from Fat 22.5%; Sat Fat 1.4g; Sod 127mg; Chol 2mg.

Trim & Terrific American Favorites (Louisiana)

Brownies in a Jar

⅔ teaspoon salt
½ plus ⅛ cup all-purpose flour
⅓ cup cocoa
½ cup all-purpose flour (mixed with ½ teaspoon baking powder)
⅔ cup firmly packed brown sugar
⅔ cup sugar
½ cup semisweet chocolate chips
½ cup chopped pecans (optional)

Layer in order given in clean quart jar: salt, ½ plus ⅛ cup flour, cocoa, ½ cup flour, brown sugar, sugar, chocolate chips, and pecans. Seal jar with lid.

Decorate jar with fabric and/or ribbon. Attach a tag (see below) to the jar with these instructions: Combine contents of this jar with 1 teaspoon vanilla, ⅔ cup vegetable oil, and 3 eggs. Pour batter into a greased 9x9-inch pan. Bake at 350° for 32–37 minutes. Yields 16–25.

Calling All Kids (Alabama)

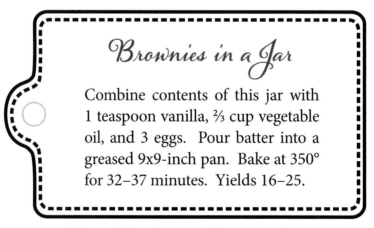

Brownies in a Jar

Combine contents of this jar with 1 teaspoon vanilla, ⅔ cup vegetable oil, and 3 eggs. Pour batter into a greased 9x9-inch pan. Bake at 350° for 32–37 minutes. Yields 16–25.

When giving these as gifts, copy and cut out this tag containing instructions. Attach one to each jar with a festive ribbon!

Rocky Road Brownies

Also called Heavenly Hash Brownies, these are a chocolate-lover's delight.

BROWNIES:

½ cup butter

2 tablespoons cocoa

2 eggs

1 cup sugar

¾ cup all-purpose flour

1 teaspoon vanilla

Pinch of salt

½ cup chopped unsalted nuts

Melt butter, and stir in cocoa. In a mixing bowl, beat eggs and add sugar. Beat in melted butter and cocoa mixture, then add flour, vanilla, and salt. Stir in nuts. Bake at 350° for 20–25 minutes in a greased and floured 8x8x2-inch pan. A toothpick inserted into center should come out almost clean.

¼ cup butter

6 tablespoons evaporated milk

3 cups or 1 pound powdered
    sugar

3 tablespoons cocoa

½ cup unsalted nuts

6 ounces miniature marshmallows
    (or 20 regular, cut in half)

While Brownies bake, mix butter, milk, powdered sugar, and cocoa in the top of a double boiler over boiling water. Stir in nuts. When Brownies are baked, spread (or place) marshmallows over them, and pour chocolate sauce on top. Cool, and cut into squares. Yields 16.

Southern Country Cooking (Kentucky)

Brownie Decadence

This recipe was made on Food Network's television show Calling All Cooks.

1 cup (2 sticks) butter or margarine	2 teaspoons vanilla
4 squares (4 ounces) unsweetened baking chocolate	1½ cups all-purpose flour
2 cups sugar	1 teaspoon baking powder
4 large eggs	1 teaspoon salt
	1 bar (4-ounces) premium white chocolate, chopped

Preheat oven to 350°. Lightly grease or coat a 9x13-inch baking pan with nonstick cooking spray. In a large saucepan, melt butter and unsweetened chocolate over low heat. Remove from heat, and mix in sugar. Add eggs and vanilla, stirring until well blended. Add flour, baking powder, and salt; stir just until mixed. Gently stir in chopped white chocolate. Spread mixture in prepared pan. Bake 25–30 minutes until brownies begin to pull away from sides of pan and center is slightly puffed. Remove from oven, and cool completely. While brownies are baking, prepare Ganache Topping. Yields 24 squares.

GANACHE TOPPING:

1 cup heavy cream	1½ cups pecans, toasted and chopped
2 cups semisweet chocolate chips	

In a medium saucepan, bring heavy cream just to a boil. Remove from heat, and add chocolate chips. Let set for a few minutes to soften chocolate. Stir until mixture is smooth. Set aside; let chocolate mixture cool and thicken, stirring occasionally, 30–45 minutes. Spread onto brownies. Sprinkle with pecans. When Ganache Topping has hardened, cut into 24 squares. Cut squares into 48 triangles, if desired. Carefully remove from pan. (Can be tightly covered and frozen up to 3 weeks.)

Confessions of a Kitchen Diva (Georgia)

Raspberry Cheesecake Brownies

BROWNIES:

4 ounces semisweet chocolate
2 ounces unsweetened chocolate
½ cup (1 stick) butter
1¼ cups sugar
3 eggs

¾ cup self-rising flour
1½ teaspoons vanilla extract
¾ teaspoon salt
1 cup seedless raspberry jam
1 tablespoon lemon juice

Heat semisweet chocolate, unsweetened chocolate, and butter in top of a double boiler over hot water until blended, stirring frequently. Remove from heat. Let stand until cool. Whisk in sugar until blended. Add eggs one at a time, whisking after each addition until smooth. Whisk in flour, vanilla, and salt until blended. Spread batter in a buttered and floured 9x13-inch baking pan. Heat jam and lemon juice in saucepan until melted, stirring frequently. Pour jam mixture evenly over prepared layer.

CREAM CHEESE TOPPING:

1 (8-ounce) package cream
  cheese, softened
⅔ cup plus 1 tablespoon sugar,
  divided
1 egg
2 teaspoons fresh lemon juice

½ teaspoon vanilla extract
¼ teaspoon salt
2 tablespoons all-purpose flour
1½ cups fresh or frozen
  raspberries

Beat cream cheese and ⅔ cup sugar in mixing bowl until light and fluffy. Beat in egg, lemon juice, vanilla, and salt. Add flour, and beat until smooth. Pour and lightly spread cream cheese mixture over prepared layer. Sprinkle with raspberries and remaining 1 tablespoon sugar. Bake in preheated 350° oven 35–40 minutes or until light brown; do not overbake. Cool in pan on wire rack. Chill, covered, 6–8 hours. Cut into squares. Yields 3–4 dozen brownies.

Provisions & Politics (Tennessee)

Editor's Extra: This old classic recipe can be made easier by microwaving the chocolates 2 minutes on HIGH, then stir pats of butter in till melted.

Kentucky Hospitality Bourbon Balls

Makes a lot. Easy to half—but you may wish you hadn't!

¼ cup bourbon
2 cups finely chopped pecans
1 cup (2 sticks) butter, softened
1 (5-ounce) can evaporated milk

3 pounds confectioners' sugar
4 cups (24 ounces) semisweet
    chocolate chips (or chocolate
    coating)

Pour bourbon over pecans in a bowl, and toss to coat. Combine butter, evaporated milk, and confectioners' sugar in a bowl; blend well. Add pecan mixture, and knead well. Roll into 1-inch balls. Place on a tray. Chill until firm.

Temper the chocolate.* Dip the balls into chocolate using a dipping fork or wooden pick, and shake off excess chocolate. Place on a tray lined with wax paper. Let stand until cool. If desried, place in individual petit four packages or mini cupcake liners. Yields about 96.

Pride of Kentucky (Kentucky)

Editor's Extra: To temper chocolate, melt ⅔ chocolate to a temperature of 118°, then add the remaining ⅓ chocolate to melted mixture, stirring until mixture has reached 88° (do not allow to cool below 78°, or process will need to be repeated). (We like to substitute 4 cups of candy coating for the semisweet chocolate chips.)

Tidewater Toffee

2 cups sugar
1 pound butter (do not substitute
   margarine)

1½ cups chopped pecans,
   toasted

Melt sugar and butter in a saucepan over medium heat. Bring to a boil, stirring often; bring temperature of mixture to hard-crack stage of 300°–310° (you must use a candy thermometer). Watch carefully and do not burn.

Stir chopped and toasted pecans into butter and sugar mixture; mix well. Pour quickly onto a lightly greased 10x15x1-inch baking pan. Cool to the touch; score top. Cool completely, and crack into pieces. Serves 12.

Toast to Tidewater (Virginia)

Peanut Brittle

1½ cups sugar
½ cup boiling water
1 cup white Karo syrup

2½ cups raw peanuts
2 tablespoons butter
1 teaspoon baking soda

Bring sugar, water, and Karo syrup to a rolling boil. Stir in peanuts. Cook until peanuts are done. Remove from heat, and stir in butter and baking soda. Mix well. Pour evenly onto buttered baking sheet. When cool, break into pieces.

The Five Star Family Book of Recipes (Alabama)

Divinity Fudge

This candy has a melt-in-your-mouth goodness.

2 cups sugar	Pinch of salt
½ cup white corn syrup	½ cup broken pecans
½ cup water	1 tablespoon vanilla extract
2 egg whites	

Combine sugar, corn syrup, and water in saucepan. Place over medium heat, and stir till dissolved. Boil without stirring, to hard-ball stage when tested in cold water, or 265°. While syrup is cooking, beat egg whites till stiff but not dry. Add salt, and the hot syrup, pouring slowly at first, and then faster, beating constantly. When mixture is stiff, beat with a wooden spoon till creamy. Add pecans, and vanilla. Pour into greased dish. Mark into 1-inch squares. Yields 24 squares.

Note: Chopped candied cherries, and pineapple may be added instead of pecans; almond extract may replace vanilla.

The Nashville Cookbook (Tennessee)

My Favorite Candy

1 pound white chocolate or candy coating	1½ cups roasted unsalted peanuts
½ cup peanut butter	1½ cups Rice Krispies
1½ cups miniature marshmallows	

Melt chocolate in 200° oven (or in microwave for 2 minutes on HIGH). Stir in peanut butter. Add remaining ingredients. Drop by teaspoonfuls onto wax paper. Let cool. Yields 6½ dozen.

Cooking with Friends–Curry Chapel (Tennessee)

Pies & Other Desserts

Nanny's Caramel Pie

When Nanny went to the kitchen and pulled out that black iron skillet, we knew we were in for a treat!

1 cup plus 2 tablespoons sugar, divided	Pinch of salt
1 tablespoon all-purpose flour	1 tablespoon very hot water
3 eggs (2 separated)	1 teaspoon vanilla
1¼ cups milk	1 tablespoon butter
	1 (8-inch) pie crust, baked

Mix ½ cup sugar with flour. Beat 1 egg plus 2 egg yolks (save whites for meringue), and add to sugar mixture. Add milk and salt, beating well with wire whisk. Set aside.

Brown ½ cup sugar in a heavy pan. It is best to do this over medium heat, allowing sugar to melt slowly. When completely dissolved, continue to cook until syrup is a golden color. (Watch out—this will burn easily if overcooked.) When sugar is browned, add 1 tablespoon very hot water, whisking constantly. Continue whisking as you slowly pour egg-milk mixture into browned sugar. Cook until thickened. Remove from heat, and add vanilla and butter. Pour into baked pie crust, and top with meringue (whip remaining egg whites with 1–2 tablespoons sugar until stiff). Bake in 350° oven until meringue is lightly browned. Cool before serving. Serves 6–8.

Family Secrets...the Best of the Delta (Mississippi)

Buttermilk Pie

1 stick margarine (melted, but
   not hot)
1⅓ cups sugar
⅓ cup all-purpose flour
3 eggs, beaten

1 teaspoon vanilla extract
1 cup buttermilk
1 deep-dish pie crust, or 2 regular
   pie crusts

Melt margarine, and stir in sugar; add flour, and mix. Stir in eggs, then vanilla. Add buttermilk, stirring well. (If using 2 regular crusts, add ¼ cup each of buttermilk, sugar, and flour to recipe.) Place crust(s) in glass pie baking dish(es) on cookie sheet for support. Pour mixture into crust(s). Don't overfill single deep-dish crust. Bake at 350° for 32–42 minutes until firm and golden brown. Cool, and serve immediately, or refrigerate for serving later. Serves 6–8.

Variation: To convert this into chocolate buttermilk pie, add several heaping tablespoons of cocoa with the buttermilk.

Let's Get Together (Mississippi)

Toasted Coconut Pie

3 eggs, beaten
1½ cups sugar
½ cup butter or margarine,
   melted
1 tablespoon plus 1 teaspoon
   lemon juice
1 teaspoon vanilla
1⅓ cups flaked coconut
1 unbaked 9-inch pastry shell
Whipped cream or topping
1 cup flaked coconut, toasted

Combine eggs, sugar, butter or margarine, lemon juice, and vanilla, mixing thoroughly. Stir in 1⅓ cups coconut. Pour filling into pastry shell. Bake at 350° for 40–45 minutes or until firm. Cool slightly before serving. Serve with dollops of whipped cream or topping, and garnish with toasted coconut. Serves 6–8.

Call to Post (Kentucky)

Editor's Extra: To easily toast coconut: Spread on a large paper plate; microwave on HIGH for 1½ minutes. Stir well. Microwave in increments of 25 seconds, stirring each time, till some has browned.

Mama's Coconut Cream Pie

¼ cup cornstarch
⅔ cup sugar (reserve 6
   tablespoons)
½ teaspoon salt
2½ cups milk

3 eggs, separated
1 teaspoon vanilla
1 cup flaked coconut, divided
1 (9-inch) pastry shell

Mix cornstarch, sugar (less reserved 6 tablespoons), and salt together in top of double boiler. Slowly stir in milk. Cook over boiling water, stirring constantly, until thick enough to mound slightly when dropped from spoon. Cover, and cook 10 minutes longer, stirring occasionally. Stir a little hot mixture into beaten egg yolks, then stir all into remaining hot mixture. Cook 2 minutes, stirring constantly. Remove from boiling water. Stir in vanilla and ¾ cup coconut. Cool to room temperature. Turn into pastry shell.

Beat egg whites until foamy. Add reserved 6 tablespoons sugar, one tablespoon at a time, beating well. Continue beating until peaks form when beater is raised. Spread meringue on top of filling, sealing edges. Sprinkle remaining ¼ cup coconut on top. Bake at 450° for 5 minutes until golden brown and coconut is toasted. Cool at room temperature (away from drafts) before refrigerating.

Note: This filling can also be used for banana pudding; just add desired amount of sliced bananas, leave out the coconut, and do not let it thicken. Also can use for cream puffs, but let thicken.

A Cookbook of Treasures (Alabama)

Chocolate Pecan Pie

This is scary good!

CRUST:

1 cup unbleached flour

7 tablespoons cold, unsalted
   butter

¼ teaspoon salt

1–3 tablespoons ice water

The Crust may be made in a food processor or by hand. If using a processor, put flour, butter, and salt in bowl, and process until it is the consistency of fine meal. Add 1 tablespoon ice water at a time, and process briefly until dough starts to form a ball. Remove from bowl, form into a ball, roll out on a well-floured board or counter, and fit into a 9-inch pie plate. Crimp edges. Preheat oven to 350°.

(If mixing by hand, put the flour, butter, and salt in a large mixing bowl, and using a pastry blender or 2 knives, cut butter into flour until it resembles coarse meal. Proceed as above.)

FILLING:

2 eggs

1 cup sugar

½ cup butter, melted

¼ cup Kentucky bourbon

¼ cup cornstarch, sifted

1 cup toasted, chopped pecans

1 cup (6 ounces) chopped
   semisweet chocolate

Beat eggs and sugar in a medium-size mixing bowl until thick and lemon-colored. Stir in butter, bourbon, and cornstarch. Sprinkle pecans on bottom of Crust. Sprinkle chocolate on top of pecans, and pour egg mixture evenly over the nuts and chocolate. Bake 45 minutes. Serve slightly warm with unsweetened whipped cream dusted with cocoa or curls of chocolate. Yields 8 servings.

Racing to the Table (Kentucky)

Honey Pecan Pie

There are as many variations for pecan pie in Louisiana as there are pastry shops. This recipe was given to me many years ago by a wonderful cook. I often wonder how wealthy she could have become, had she sold this dessert.

¼ pound butter
1 cup sugar
3 eggs, beaten
½ cup corn syrup
½ cup honey
½ teaspoon lemon juice

1 teaspoon vanilla
1 cup chopped pecans
Pinch of cinnamon
Pinch of nutmeg
1 (9-inch) uncooked pie shell

Preheat oven to 425°. In a heavy bottom sauté pan, brown butter over medium-high heat. Do not burn. Remove, and allow to cool slightly. In a large mixing bowl, combine sugar, eggs, syrup, and honey. Using a wire whisk, blend all ingredients well. Add the brown butter, lemon juice, vanilla, and pecans. Season with cinnamon and nutmeg. Continue to whip until all ingredients are well blended. Pour into pie shell, and bake on center rack of oven for 10 minutes. Then reduce temperature to 375°, and bake for 35 minutes. Remove, and allow to cool.

The Evolution of Cajun & Creole Cuisine (Louisiana)

Sweet Potato Pie

For years my sister's favorite pie was pumpkin . . . she didn't know that my mom told her sweet potato pie was pumpkin pie. She couldn't understand why other people's pumpkin pie just didn't taste like Mom's!

2 cups cooked sweet potatoes,
    mashed (about 2 medium)
1 cup sugar
2 eggs, beaten
¼ cup butter, melted

1 teaspoon vanilla
¾ cup milk
1 teaspoon cinnamon
¼ teaspoon nutmeg
1 unbaked pie shell

Mix all ingredients well, and pour into pie shell. Bake at 350° for 60 minutes or until tests done.

Gritslickers (North Carolina)

Editor's Extra: We like to serve with a few squirts of whipped cream right out of the can . . . makes it even *more* delicious.

Company's Coming Peach Pie

1 (8- or 9-inch) pie shell,
    unbaked
1 tablespoon butter, melted
2 teaspoons vanilla extract
1 (8-ounce) package cream
    cheese, softened

¼ cup sugar
¼ cup sour cream
½ cup apricot preserves, divided
1 (16-ounce) can sliced red
    freestone peaches, drained

Brush pie shell with butter. Bake according to package directions; let stand until cool. In a blender or food processor, process vanilla, cream cheese, sugar, sour cream, and ¼ cup preserves until smooth. Pour into baked pie shell. Arrange peaches artfully in a spoke pattern over top. Drizzle remaining ¼ cup preserves (may have to heat slightly) over peaches. Chill in refrigerator. Serves 6.

Some Assembly Required (Georgia)

Crisp Crust Apple Pie

FILLING:

5 medium apples (Red or Golden Delicious)
1½ cups sugar
1 teaspoon all-purpose flour
1 teaspoon cinnamon (more or less depending on taste)
½ cup water

Slice apples thin into an oblong baking dish. Mix together sugar, flour, and cinnamon; sprinkle over apples. Pour water over mixture.

CRUST:

2½ cups self-rising flour
½ teaspoon salt
⅔ cup shortening
About ½ cup ice water
¾ cup sugar
1 teaspoon cinnamon
1 stick (½ cup) butter or margarine, sliced

Mix flour and salt; cut in shortening. Add enough water to hold dough together. Roll between sheets of wax paper. Place on top of Filling. Sprinkle with sugar and cinnamon (mixed together). Dot with butter. Bake at 400° until Crust is browned and apples are tender. (When I have been in a rush, I have substituted 2 frozen pie shells for Crust).

The Apple Barn Cookbook (Tennessee)

Strawberry Splendor Mile High Pie

The crust complements the delicious strawberry taste!

CRUST:

1 cup all-purpose flour
¼ cup firmly packed light
  brown sugar

½ cup butter, melted
½ cup finely chopped pecans

Preheat oven to 350°. In a large mixing bowl, combine all Crust ingredients until blended. Spread thinly onto an ungreased baking sheet. Bake 15 minutes, stirring occasionally. Cool slightly. Stir to crumble. Reserve ½ cup crumb mixture for garnish. Press remaining warm crumb mixture into a lightly buttered 9-inch glass pie plate. Cool.

FILLING:

1 (10-ounce) package frozen
  strawberries with syrup,
  thawed
2 teaspoons freshly squeezed
  lemon juice

1 cup sugar
2 egg whites
1 (8-ounce) carton whipping
  cream, whipped

Using an electric mixer, combine strawberries, lemon juice, sugar, and egg whites. Beat on high speed 15 minutes until mixture is very stiff. (Beating is the secret!) Fold in whipped cream by hand. Turn Filling into prepared Crust. Sprinkle reserved crumb mixture over top. Freeze overnight before serving; serve frozen.

Bevelyn Blair's Everyday Pies (Georgia)

Editor's Extra: How long you beat it and how quickly you get the the high pie into the freezer will determine this pie's height. But no matter, it's *goooooood.*

Bessie's Peanut Butter Pie

CHOCOLATE CRUST:

1 (6-ounce) package semisweet
  chocolate chips

⅓ cup margarine or butter
2½ cups oven-toasted rice cereal

In heavy saucepan over low heat, melt chocolate chips with margarine or butter. Remove from heat; gently stir in cereal until completely coated. Press into bottom and up side of greased 9-inch pie plate. Chill 30 minutes.

PEANUT BUTTER FILLING:

1 (8-ounce) package cream
  cheese, softened
1 (14-ounce) can sweetened
  condensed milk
¾ cup peanut butter

1 teaspoon vanilla extract
½ pint whipping cream, whipped
  (or 8 ounces whipped topping)
1–2 teaspoons chocolate-flavored
  syrup

In large bowl, beat cheese until fluffy; beat in condensed milk and peanut butter until smooth. Stir in vanilla. Fold in whipped cream. Turn into crust. Drizzle syrup over top of pie; gently swirl with spoon. Chill 4 hours or until set. Serves 8–10.

Hudson's Cookbook (South Carolina)

Editor's Extra: We topped our pie with peanuts instead of chocolate syrup.

No-Bake Key Lime Pie

1 (8-ounce) package cream cheese, softened
1 (14-ounce) can sweetened condensed milk
3 ounces Key lime juice
1 graham cracker pie shell, baked
Sliced strawberries, kiwi, or other fresh fruit, or fruit pie filling
Whipped cream

Blend cream cheese and condensed milk (it will have some tiny lumps of cheese). Add lime juice, one ounce at a time; blend well with each addition. Pour into pie shell, and chill.

At serving time, top with one or more of the fruit slices or pie filling and whipped cream.

The Cruising K.I.S.S. Cookbook II (Florida)

Fried Pies

A southern specialty!

1 teaspoon salt
1 teaspoon baking powder
2 cups all-purpose flour, sifted
2 tablespoons solid shortening
1 egg yolk
4 tablespoons sugar
½ cup milk
1 (6- to 7-ounce) package dried fruit, cooked and sweetened
Powdered sugar

In a large bowl, sift salt and baking powder with measured flour. Blend in shortening. Combine egg yolk, sugar, and milk. Stir into flour mixture. Roll out on a floured board to ¼-inch thickness. Cut into circles 4–5 inches in diameter. Spread a small amount of cooked and sweetened dried fruit on half of each round. Moisten edges, and fold crust over filling. Seal edges with a fork dipped in flour. Fry in deep fat at 360° until browned. Drain on absorbent paper, and sprinkle with powdered sugar.

A Taste of Georgia (Georgia)

Editor's Extra: To plump dried fruit, bring 2 cups water to a boil and add dried fruit; simmer about 20 minutes. Add a cup of sugar. Good to add a tad of butter and a shake of cinnamon, if you like.

Georgia Blackberry Cobbler

3–4 cups blackberries
¾ cup sugar
3 tablespoons all-purpose flour

1½ cups water
1 tablespoon lemon juice

Place berries in a lightly greased shallow 2-quart baking dish. In a bowl, combine sugar and flour; stir in water and lemon juice. Pour mixture over berries; bake at 425° for 15 minutes.

CRUST:

1¾ cups all-purpose flour
2 teaspoons baking powder
¾ teaspoon salt
2–3 tablespoons sugar
¼ cup shortening

¼ cup plus 2 tablespoons
  whipping cream
¼ cup plus 2 tablespoons
  buttermilk
2 tablespoons butter, melted

Combine first 4 ingredients in a bowl. Cut in shortening with pastry blender until mixture resembles coarse meal; stir in whipping cream and buttermilk. Knead dough 4–5 times; roll out on a lightly floured surface. Cut dough to fit baking dish. Place Crust over hot berries; brush with butter. Bake at 425° for 20–30 minutes or until golden brown. Serve warm with ice cream, if desired. Yields 6–8 servings.

Our Best Home Cooking (Georgia)

Alabama "Blue Ribbon" Banana Pudding

¾ cup sugar
Dash of salt
¼ cup all-purpose flour
3 egg yolks, beaten (reserve
   whites)

1 tablespoon vanilla
2 cups half-and-half
15 vanilla wafers
2–4 bananas, sliced

Combine sugar, salt, and flour; add to egg yolks and vanilla in a double boiler. Slowly add half-and-half, stirring frequently. Heat until it thickens. Layer wafers and banana slices in 1½-quart baking dish. Add pudding.

MERINGUE:
3 egg whites (reserved)
2 dashes cream of tartar

6 tablespoons sugar
½ teaspoon vanilla

Beat egg whites and cream of tartar for 2 minutes. Slowly add sugar and vanilla, and beat until very stiff. Spread over pudding, and bake at 350° until Meringue is golden brown, about 5 minutes. Serves 4–6.

Capitol Cooking (Alabama)

Not Your Ordinary Banana Pudding

2 (7¼-ounce) bags Pepperidge
  Farm Chessmen cookies,
  divided
6–8 bananas, sliced
2 cups milk
1 (5-ounce) box French vanilla
  instant pudding

1 (8-ounce) package cream cheese,
  softened
1 (14-ounce) can sweetened
  condensed milk
1 (12-ounce) container frozen
  whipped topping, thawed

Line bottom of a 9x13-inch dish with 1 bag of cookies, and layer bananas on top. In a bowl, combine milk and pudding mix, and blend well using a mixer. In another bowl, combine cream cheese and condensed milk, and mix until smooth. Fold whipped topping into cream cheese mixture. Add cream cheese mixture to pudding mixture, and stir until well blended. Pour mixture over cookies and bananas. Top pudding mixture with remaining bag of cookies. Refrigerate at least 2 hours before serving. Serves 6–8.

G. W. Carver Family Recipes (Virginia)

Bread Pudding with Rum Sauce

4 cups milk
2 cups sugar
4 eggs, beaten
1 tablespoon vanilla extract

1 cup raisins
1–1½ cups chopped peeled apples
1 (16-ounce) loaf dry French bread,
   torn into bite-size pieces

Beat milk, sugar, and eggs in mixer bowl until blended. Stir in vanilla, apples, and raisins. Pour over bread in bowl; mix well. Let stand until bread absorbs milk, stirring occasionally. Spoon into greased 9x9-inch baking pan. May chill at this point, and bake just before serving. Bake at 350° for 30–40 minutes or until pudding tests done.

RUM SAUCE:
2 eggs
¼ cup rum

1 cup confectioners' sugar
1 cup whipping cream, whipped

Beat eggs in saucepan. Add rum and confectioners' sugar; mix well. Cook over low heat until of desired consistency. Remove from heat; cool slightly; fold into whipped cream. Serve warm bread pudding with Rum Sauce or vanilla ice cream. Yields 10 servings.

Note: May substitute rum extract for rum.

Home Sweet Habitat (Georgia)

Frosty Strawberry Squares

1 cup sifted all-purpose flour
¼ cup brown sugar
½ cup chopped walnuts or
   pecans
½ cup butter, melted
2 egg whites

1 cup sugar
2 cups sliced fresh strawberries, or
   1 (10-ounce) package frozen,
   partially thawed
2 teaspoons lemon juice
1 cup heavy cream, whipped

Stir together first 4 ingredients; spread evenly in shallow baking pan. Bake 20 minutes in 350° oven, stirring occasionally. Sprinkle ⅔ of this crumbled mixture in a 9x13-inch baking pan. Combine egg whites, sugar, berries, and lemon juice in a large bowl. Beat at high speed till stiff peaks form, about 10 minutes. Fold in whipped cream. Top with remaining crumbled mixture. Freeze 6 hours or overnight. Cut into squares. Top with fresh strawberries. Yields 15 squares.

Woman's Exchange Cookbook I (Tennessee)

Strawberries Rebecca

2 quarts fresh strawberries,
   washed and stemmed
2 cups sour cream
1 cup light brown sugar

1 tablespoon vanilla
1 tablespoon cinnamon
Fresh mint for garnish

Place strawberries in large bowl or small dessert dishes. Combine sour cream, light brown sugar, vanilla, and cinnamon. Spoon over strawberries; garnish with mint. Sauce can be made ahead and refrigerated. Serves 8.

Simply Florida . . . Strawberries (Florida)

Carolina Trifle

½ (9-inch) yellow cake layer,
    divided
¾ cup grated coconut, divided
1 (3-ounce) package vanilla
    instant pudding

3 cups milk
1 teaspoon vanilla
1 (8-ounce) carton nondairy
    whipped topping

Crumble ½ of cake into a 6x10-inch casserole. Sprinkle with ¼ cup coconut. Make pudding according to directions, using milk and vanilla as directed. Pour ½ of pudding immediately over crumbled cake and coconut. Quickly crumble remaining cake over pudding, and sprinkle with ¼ cup coconut. Pour remaining pudding over cake and coconut. Spread whipped topping over pudding; sprinkle with remaining ¼ cup coconut. Chill at least 2 hours before serving. Serves 8.

Strictly for Boys (South Carolina)

Cherry Trifle

An elegance-with-ease dessert! Prepare and serve in a glass bowl, so everyone can enjoy its beauty. If you wish, make it hours before serving.

1 package ladyfingers
Jelly (your favorite)
1 (3-ounce) package vanilla
    pudding mix (not instant)

1 (16-ounce) can pitted dark sweet
    cherries, drained
Whipped cream, if desired

Split ladyfingers; spread tops and bottoms with jelly; sandwich back together. Place ladyfingers in bottom and around sides of a medium glass bowl or round casserole. (Stand them up like children holding hands and walking around.)

Cook pudding mixture, following package directions. Pour some of the pudding over ladyfingers in bottom of bowl. Arrange a layer of cherries on top of pudding. Repeat layers again. Top with cherries and whipped cream. Store in refrigerator till serving time. Serves 8.

Home Cooking in a Hurry (Tennessee)

Chocolate Tower

1 (17-ounce) package fudge
brownie mix

2 (3-ounce) packages chocolate
instant mousse mix

6 (1.4-ounce) chocolate toffee bars,
chopped

16 ounces whipped topping

Prepare brownie mix according to package directions; cool completely. Crumble brownies into a bowl. Prepare chocolate mousse mix according to package directions.

Layer crumbled brownies, chocolate mousse, chopped toffee bars, and whipped topping, half at a time, in a trifle dish. Serve immediately or chill, covered, until ready to serve. Yields 10–12 servings.

Open House: A Culinary Tour (Tennessee)

Sleeping Meringue

1 angel food cake, sliced
   horizontally into halves
6 egg whites
¼ teaspoon salt
½ teaspoon cream of tartar
1½ cups sugar
1 teaspoon vanilla
1 cup whipping cream
2 cups sliced fruit, such as
   strawberries, peaches,
   blueberries, or a combination

Preheat oven to 450°. Place half the angel food cake in a buttered deep-dish springform pan with a hole. Beat egg whites in a large bowl until stiff peaks form; add salt and cream of tartar while beating. Add sugar and vanilla gradually; beat 15 minutes. Pour meringue over cake half in pan; place in oven. Turn off heat, and go to bed (8–10 hours).

Remove dessert from pan to a serving plate just before serving time. Whip whipping cream in a bowl, and spread over top of dessert. Garnish with fruit. Yields 8–10 servings.

Note: There is half a cake left over, so you can double the recipe and make two desserts, or just nibble on that extra half of the cake. I consider that a cook's benefit.

Celebrate Virginia! (Virginia)

Homemade Peach Ice Cream

3 cups sugar
4 eggs, beaten
1 quart milk
1 tablespoon vanilla
1 (14-ounce) can sweetened
   condensed milk
2 (12-ounce) cans evaporated
   milk

1 quart sweetened sliced
   peaches
Sugar to taste
Whole milk
Ice
Rock salt

Combine first 4 ingredients, and cook on top of stove until it thickens. Remove from heat, and cool. Add condensed milk and evaporated milk. Blend peaches in blender, and add sugar to taste. Add to milk mixture. Pour into 6-quart ice cream churn, and finish filling with whole milk. Fill churn with ice and rock salt, and churn.

Red Oak Recipes (Georgia)

Buttermilk Ice Cream

(Glace au Petit-Lait)

Mrs. Sis Lipson provided me with this very old recipe for buttermilk ice cream as it was served by a now-closed Pensacola ice cream parlor.

1 quart buttermilk
½ pint cream
1 (14-ounce) can sweetened
   condensed milk

1 (12-ounce) can evaporated milk
½ cup lemon juice
½ cup sugar

Combine buttermilk, cream, milks, vanilla, lemon juice, and sugar. Place in ice cream freezer can, and freeze according to directions.

Optional: Replace part or all the lemon juice with 1 cup crushed pineapple.

Gourmet Cooking II (Florida)

Amy's Ice Cream Sandwich Dessert

3 milk chocolate candy bars,
3 Skor candy bars
⅓ cup Kahlúa

1 (16-ounce) carton whipped
**   topping**
24 ice cream sandwiches

Chop candy bars; combine and set aside. In a mixing bowl, gently fold Kahlúa into whipped topping. Arrange half the ice cream sandwiches in a 9x13-inch pan. Spread half whipped topping mixture over sandwiches, and sprinkle with half the candy bar mixture. Repeat layers of ice cream sandwiches, whipped topping mixture, and candy bar mixture. Freeze for 6 hours or longer before serving. Yields 12 servings.

Calling All Cooks, Four (Alabama)

Editor's Extra: For a pretty presentation, after freezing, cut out round servings, place them in wine glasses, and garnish each with a chocolate square and a cherry.

List of Contributors

Cajun Crawfish Cornbread

Listed below are the cookbooks that have contributed recipes to the *Hall of Fame of Southern Recipes*, along with copyright, author, publisher, city and state. The information in parentheses indicates the Best of the Best cookbook in which the recipe originally appeared.

Absolutely á la Carte ©1999 by Charlotte Walton, Skelton, Cleveland, MS (Mississippi)

Accent One ©1985 Accent Enterprises, Inc., by Frank Simpson, Jr., Bentonia, MS (Mississippi)

The Alabama Heritage Cookbook ©1984 Heritage Publications, Birmingham, AL (Alabama)

Aliant Cooks for Education ©2004 Morris Press Cookbooks, by Aliant Bank, Alexander City, AL (Alabama)

The Apple Barn Cookbook ©1983 The Apple Barn, and Cider Mill, Sevierville, TN (Tennessee)

Apron Strings ©1983 by The Women's Committee of The Richmond Symphony, Richmond, VA (Virginia)

Arkansas Favorites Cookbook ©1991 J, and J Collections, Hot Springs, AR (Arkansas)

Atlanta Cooknotes ©1982 Junior League of Atlanta, GA (Georgia)

Bay Tables ©1999 Junior League of Mobile, Inc, Mobile, AL (Alabama)

The Belle Grove Plantation Cookbook ©1986 by Belle Grove, Inc., Middleton, VA (Virginia)

Best Kept Secrets, by Homeland Park Fire Department, anderson, SC (South Carolina)

The Best of the Bushel ©1987 The Junior League of Charlottesville, VA (Virginia)

Bethel Food Bazaar II ©1988 Bethel United Methodist Women, Spartanburg, SC (South Carolina)

Betty is Still "Winking" at Cooking, by Betty J. Winkler, Little Rock, AR (Arkansas)

Bevelyn Blair's Everyday Pies ©2000 by Bevelyn Blair, Columbus, GA (Georgia)

Beyond Cotton Country ©1999 Junior League of Morgan County, Decatur, AL (Alabama)

Bluegrass Winners ©1985 Garden Club of Lexington, KY (Kentucky)

Bon Appétit, by Pat Gunn, and Amy Horner, S & S Enterprises, Enterprise, AL (Alabama)

Bountiful Blessings, by DeKalb Parish United Methodist Churches, Daleville, MS (Mississippi)

Bountiful Blessings, by Macedonia Evangelical Lutheran Church, Prosperity, SC (South Carolina)

Bountiful Blessings from the Bauknight Table, by H. Felder & Margaret D. Bauknight Family, Central, SC (South Carolina)

Bravo ©1984 The Greensboro Symphony Guild, Greensboro, NC (North Carolina)

By Special Request © Leu Wilder, Shreveport, LA (Louisiana)

Cajun Cooking for Beginners ©1996 Acadian House Publishing, Lafayette, LA (Louisiana)

Cajun Men Cook ©1994 Beaver Club of Lafayette, LA (Louisiana)

Call to Post ©1977 Lexington Hearing & Speech Center, Lexington, KY (Kentucky)

Calling All Cooks ©1982 Telephone Pioneers of America, Alabama Chapter #34, Birmingham, AL (Alabama)

Calling All Cooks III ©1994 Telephone Pioneers of America, Alabama Chapter #34, Birmingham, AL (Alabama)

Calling All Cooks IV ©2000 Telephone Pioneers of America, Alabama Chapter #34, Birmingham, AL (Alabama)

Calling All Kids ©2002 Telephone Pioneers of America, Alabama Chapter #34, Birmingham, AL (Alabama)

Calypso Café ©1999 Wimmer Companies, by Bob Epstein, Memphis, TN (Tennessee)

Capitol Cooking, by Alabama Legislative Club, Clanton, AL (Alabama)

Catering to Charleston ©2004 Hamby Catering, by Frances Ellison Hamby, Charleston, SC (South Carolina)

Celebrate Virginia! ©2002 by James A. Crutchfield, Rowena Fullinwider, and Winette Sparkman Jeffery, Rowena's, Inc., Norfolk, VA (Virginia)

Celebrations ©1999 Telephone Pioneers of America, Alabama Chapter #34, Birmingham, AL (Alabama)

Charleston Receipts ©1950 The Junior League of Charleston, SC (South Carolina)

Christmas Memories ©2001 by Jeannine B. Browning, Melbourne, FL (Florida)

Civil War Period Cookery ©2003 by Robert W. Pelton, West Conshohocken, PA (Tennessee)

Coastal Carolina Cooking ©1986 The University of North Carolina Press, by Nancy Davis, and Kathy Hurt, Chapel Hill, NC (North Carolina)

Collard Greens, Watermelons, and "Miss" Charlotte's Pie ©1993 Swansboro United Methodist Women, Swansboro, NC (North Carolina)

Confessions of a Kitchen Diva ©2003 Happicook, Inc., by Claudine Destino, Roswell, GA (Georgia)

The Colonel's Inn Caterers'—Tallahassee Historical Cookbook ©1984 Colonel's Inn Caterers, by Delia Appleyard Mickler & Carolyde Phillips O'Bryan, Tallahassee, FL (Florida)

A Cookbook of Treasures, by Guine Methodist Church (Alabama)

Cookin' on Island Time, by Palm Island Estates Association, Inc, Grove City, FL (Florida)

Cooking on the Coast ©1994 by Rose Annette O'Keefe, Ocean Springs, MS (Mississippi)

Cooking with 257, by Boy Scout Troop 257, North Port, FL (Florida)

Cooking with Friends, by Curry Chapel UMC, Nameless, TN (Tennessee)

The Cotton Country Collection ©1972 Junior Charity League , Monroe, LA (Louisiana)

Country Club Cooks, by Spanish Lakes Country Club Homeowners Association, Ft. Pierce, FL (Florida)

Crab Chatter ©1964 Lewis, and Lewis, by Mildred, and Gennie Lewis, Brunswick, GA (Georgia)

The Crowning Recipes of Kentucky ©1986 Madonna Smith Echols, Marathon International Book Company, Madison, IN (Kentucky)

The Cruising K.I.S.S. Cookbook II ©2003 by Corrine C. Kanter, by SAILco Press, Inc., Marathon, FL (Florida)

Culinary Arts & Crafts ©1984 The Park Maitland School, Inc., Maitland, FL (Florida)

Culinary Classics, by Atlanta City Church's Creative Arts Dept., Fairburn, GA (Georgia)

Delightfully Southern ©1996 River Oaks Publications, by Dot Gibson, Waycross, GA (Georgia)

Dining Under the Carolina Moon ©2005 by Deborah Baker Covington, Beaufort, SC (South Carolina)

Dinner on the Diner ©1983 Junior League of Chattanooga, TN (Tennessee)

Down Here Men Don't Cook ©1984 Southern Images, Jackson, MS (Mississippi)

Down Home Dining in Mississippi ©1999 Mississippi Homemaker Volunteers, Inc., Water Valley, MS (Mississippi)

Endless Praise Dishes, by Endless Praise Ministries, Theodore, AL (Alabama)

The Essential Catfish Cookbook ©2001 by Janet Cope, and Shannon Harper, by Pineapple Press, Inc., Sarasota, FL (Florida)

The Evolution of Cajun & Creole Cuisine ©1989 Chef John Folse & Co., Gonzales, LA (Louisiana)

Faithfully Charleston ©2001 St. Michael's Episcopal Church, Charleston, SC (South Carolina)

The Farmer's Daughters ©1987 S-M-L, Inc, by Flora R. Sisemore, Martha R. Merritt, and Mary R. Mayfield, DeWitt, AR (Arkansas)

Family Favorites, by Catholic Daughters of the America's #2388, Westlake, LA (Louisiana)

Family Secrets...the Best of the Delta ©1990 Lee Academy, Clarksdale, MS (Mississippi)

Family Traditions, by Esta White Freeland, Mer Rouge, LA (Louisiana)

Favorite Recipes: Bayside Baptist Church ©2004 Bayside Baptist Church, Virginia Beach, VA (Virginia)

Feast, and Fellowship ©1985 Feast, and Fellowship, Inc., by St. Francis Guild, Cathedral of St. Philip, Atlanta, GA (Georgia)

Feasts of Eden ©1990 Apple Cooks, Inc, by August House Publishers, Little Rock, AR (Arkansas)

Feeding the Flock, by St. Joseph Catholic Church, Pensacola, FL (Florida)

Festival Cookbook ©1983 Humphreys Academy Patrons, Belzoni, MS (Mississippi)

Fillies Flavours ©1984 The Fillies Inc., Louisville, KY (Kentucky)

Fine Dining Georgia Style ©2005 by John M. Bailey, Quail Ridge Press, Brandon, MS (Georgia)

First Come, First Served...In Savannah ©2001 St., andrews School, by St., andrew's School PTO, Savannah, GA (Georgia)

The Five Star Family Book of Recipes, by Five Star Credit Union, Dothan, AL (Alabama)

Florence Cook Book, by Trinity Episcopal Churchwomen, Florence, AL (Alabama)

Florida Flavors ©1984 The Environmental Studies Council, Inc., Jensen Beach, FL (Florida)

Food, Family, and Friendships ©1996 Darden, and Proffitt , by Mary M. Darden, and Margaret T. Proffitt, Virginia Beach, VA (Virginia)

From Black Tie to Blackeyed Peas ©2000 by Irving Victor, M.D., Savannah, GA (Georgia)

From Our House to Yours © Habitat for Humanity International, Shelton, CT (Georgia)

G.W. Carver Family Recipes, by G.W. Carber Elementary School, Salem, VA (Virginia)

Game Gourmet ©1999 The Wimmer Companies, by Dr. William M. McKell, Memphis, TN (Mississippi)

Gibson/Goree Family Favorites, by Gibson/Goree Family of Choctaw County, Birmingham, AL (Alabama)

Gourmet Cooking II ©1985 Earl Peyroux, by Peyroux Enterprises, Inc., Pensacola, FL (Florida)

The Grace of Patti's ©2000 Patti's Publishers, by Chip Tullar, Grand Rivers, KY (Kentucky)

Gracious Goodness . . . Charleston! ©1991 BEHS Endowment Fund, Charleston, SC (South Carolina)

Granny's Kitchen, by Theone L. Neel, Bastian, VA (Virginia)

Granny's Taste of Christmas ©2006 by Dianne C. Evans, Charolotte, NC (North Carolina)

Gran's Gems, by Jane Rayburn Hardin, Birmingham, AL (Mississippi)

A Great Taste of Arkansas ©1986 Southern Flavors, Inc, by Southern Flavors, Inc., Pine Bluff, AR (Arkansas)

The Great Cookbook ©1986 Altrusa Club of Greater Gadsden, AL (Alabama)

Gritslickers ©2005 by Lisa Shively Cookbooks, by Lisa Lofton Shively, Eden, NC (North Carolina)

Hallmark's Collection of Home Tested Recipes, by Freeda Rogers Hallmark, Tuscaloosa, AL (Alabama)

Heart & Soul Cookbook ©2004 Women's Ministries, Greenville, AL (Alabama)

Heart of the Palms ©1982 The Junior League of the Palm Beaches, FL (Florida)

Heaven in a Pot, by Wesley United Methodist Women, Marco Island, FL (Florida)

A Heritage of Good Tastes, by Arkansas Post Museum State Park, Gillett, AR (Arkansas)

Historic Spanish Point, by Gulf Coast Heritage Association, Inc., Osprey, FL (Florida)

Holiday Delights ©1997 River Oaks Publications, by Dot Gibson, Waycross, GA (Georgia)

Home Again, Home Again ©2004 The Junior League of Owensboro, KY (Kentucky)

Home Cooking in a Hurry ©1985 Broadman Press, by Sarah Howell, Nashville, TN (Tennessee)

Home Sweet Habitat © Habitat for Humanity International, Shelton, CT (Georgia)

Hudson's Cookbook ©1982 by Brain & Gloria Carmines, Hilton Head Island, SC (South Carolina)

Irondale Café Original Whistlestop Cookbook ©1995 by Mary Jo Smith McMichael, by Original Whistlestop Café, Irondale, AL (Alabama)

Kay Ewing's Cooking School Cookbook ©1994 Kay Ewing, Baton Rouge, LA (Louisiana)

Kentucky Cook Book ©2000 Golden West Publishers, Phoenix, AZ (Kentucky)

The Kentucky Derby Museum Cook Book ©1986 Kentucky Derby Museum Corporation, Louisville, KY (Kentucky)

Kentucky Kitchens Volume I ©1989 Telephone Pioneers of America, Kentucky Chapter #32, Louisville, KY (Kentucky)

Key Ingredients ©2002 Le Bonheaur Children's Medical Center, Memphis, TN (Tennessee)

Koinonia Cooking ©1982 Elaine S. Mynatt, Knoxville, TN (Tennessee)

Korner's Folly Cookbook ©1977 Beth Tartan, and Fran Parker, Kinston, NC (North Carolina)

Kum' Ona' Granny's Table, by Senior Citizens Retirement Facility, Montgomery, AL (Alabama)

Lagniappe, by Patsy Switzer, Ocean Springs, MS (Mississippi)

Let's Get Together ©2001 Junior Auxiliary of Clinton, Clinton, MS (Mississippi)

Linen Napkins to Paper Plates ©1988 Junior Auxiliary of Clarksville, TN (Tennessee)

Louisiana's Original Creole Seafood Recipes, by Tony Chachere, Creole Foods of Opelousas, LA (Louisiana)

Madison County Cookery ©1980 Madison County Chamber of Commerce, Canton, MS (Mississippi)

Magic ©1982 The Junior League of Birmingham, AL (Alabama)

Mama's Recipes, and Others Cookbook ©1976 June Thompson Medlin, Lake Junaluska, NC (North Carolina)

Margaritaville Cookbook ©1984 VIPCO, by Ruth Perez, and Brenda Vidal, Key West, FL (Florida)

Minnie Pearl Cooks ©1970 Minnie Pearl, Nashville, TN (Tennessee)

Mississippi Stars Cookbook, by South Pontotoc Attendance Center PTO, Pontotoc, MS (Mississippi)

Mountain Country Cooking ©1996 by Mark F. Sohn, St. Martin's Press, New York, NY (Kentucky)

Mountain Laurel Encore ©1984 Bell County Extension Homemakers, Pineville, KY (Kentucky)

My Mother Cooked My Way Through Harvard With These Creole Recipes ©1977 Oscar A. Rogers, Jackson, MS (Mississippi)

The Nashville Cookbook ©1976, 1977 Nashville Area Home Economics Assn., Nashville, TN (Tennessee)

Nibbles Cooks Cajun ©1983, by Suzie Stephens, Fayatteville, AR (Arkansas)

North Carolina Cook Book ©1999 Golden West Publishers, by Janice Therese Mancuso, Phoenix, AZ (North Carolina)

Not By Bread Alone Cookbook, by Mt. Olivet United Methodist Church, Bastian, VA (Virginia)

Open House: A Culinary Tour ©2002 Junior League of Murfreesboro, TN (Tennessee)

Our Best Home Cooking ©2001 by Judith C. Dryer, Norcross, GA (Georgia)

Our Favorite Recipes, Volume II, by Mt. View Baptist Church, Trinity, AL (Alabama)

Out of Our League ©1978 Junior League of Greensboro, NC (North Carolina)

Out of this World ©1983 The Oak Hill School Parents' Assn., Nashville, TN (Tennessee)

Palm Beach Entertains ©1976 The Junior League of the Palm Beaches, FL (Florida)

Palmetto Hospitality Inn Style ©1994 by Tracy M. Winters, and Phyllis Y Winters, Greensburg, IN (South Carolina)

Paris Winners, by Paris/Bourbon County Chamber of Commerce, Paris, KY (Kentucky)

The Pick of the Crop ©1978 North Sunflower PTA, Drew, MS (Mississippi)

Pleasant Grove Baptist Church Cookbook, by Pleasant Grove Baptist Church, Red Level, AL (Alabama)

Pon Top Edisto ©1997 Trinity Episcopal Church, Edisto Island, SC (South Carolina)

Pride of Kentucky ©2003 by Kentucky Extension Association of Family, and Consumer Sciences, Owingsville, KY (Kentucky)

Prime Meridian ©2001 Lamar Foundation, by Lamar School, Meridian, MS (Mississippi)

Provisions & Politics ©2003 James K. Polk Memorial Association, Columbia, TN (Tennessee)

Racing to the Table ©2002 The Blood-Horse, Inc., by Margaret Guthrie, Lexington, KY (Kentucky)

The Rappahannock Seafood Cookbook ©1984 Rappahannock Community College Educational Foundation, Inc., Warsaw, VA (Virginia)

Recipe Jubilee ©1964 The Junior League of Mobile, AL (Alabama)

Recipes, and Reminiscences of New Orleans II ©1971 Parents Club of Ursuline Academy Inc., Ursuline Convent Cookbook, Metairie, LA (Louisiana)

Recipes from the Heart of Branch, by Branch Baptist Church (Youth), Morton, MS (Mississippi)

Red Oak Recipes, by Frances G. Womack, Tifton, GA (Georgia)

River Road Recipes III ©1994 The Junior League of Baton Rouge, LA (Louisiana)

A River's Course ©2005 Junior Charity League of Shelby, NC (North Carolina)

A Samford Celebration Cookbook, by Samford University Auxiliary, Birmingham, AL (Alabama)

Savor the Moment ©2000 The Junior League of Boca Raton, FL (Florida)

Savor the Spirit ©2002 Alabama Society, United States Daughters of 1812, Birmingham, AL (Alabama)

Seaboard to Sideboard ©1998 The Junior League of Wilmington, NC (North Carolina)

Secret Recipes, by Humane Society of Wilkes, North Wilkesboro, NC (North Carolina)

Secrets of The Original Don's Seafood & Steakhouse ©1996 Don's Seafood & Steakhouse of Louisiana, Inc., Lafayette, LA (Louisiana)

Simply Florida . . . Strawberries, by Florida Strawberry Grower's Association, Plant City, FL (Florida)

Sisters' Secrets, Beta Sigma Phi, Ville Platte, LA (Louisiana)

Smokehouse Ham, Spoon Bread, & Scuppernong Wine ©1998 by Joseph Dabney, Nashville, TN (Tennessee)

Smoky Mountain Magic ©1960 Junior League of Johnson City, TN (Tennessee)

Some Assembly Required ©2004 by Lee J. Chadwick, Meridian International Publishing, Alpharetta, GA (Georgia)

Somethin's Cookin' at LG&E ©1986 LG&E Employees Association, Inc., Louisville, KY (Kentucky)

The South Carolina Cook Book ©1954 University of South Carolina Press, Columbia, SC (South Carolina)

Southern Country Cooking ©1992 by Mark F. Sohn, Penfield Press, Iowa City, IA (Kentucky)

Southern Scrumptious ©2002 by Betty Brandon Sims, Decatur, AL (Alabama)

Southern Vegetable Cooking ©1981 Sandlapper Publishing Co., Inc., Orangeburg, SC (South Carolina)

Splendor in the Bluegrass ©2000 Junior League of Louisville, KY (Kentucky)

Straight from the Galley Past & Present, by Ladies Auxiliary of Bay Waveland Yacht Club, Bay St. Louis, MS (Mississippi)

Strictly for Boys ©1980 by Betty L. Waskiewicz, Beaufort, SC (South Carolina)

Taste Buds ©1985 Winslow, Woverton, Komegay, Hertford, NC (North Carolina)

A Taste of Georgia ©1977 Newman Junior Service League, Inc., Newman, GA (Georgia)

A Taste of Heaven, by Crestwood Baptist Church, Frankfort, KY (Kentucky)

A Taste of the Holidays ©1988 Dot Gibson Publications, Waycross, GA (Georgia)

A Taste of the Outer Banks II, by Bea Basnight, and Gail Midgett, B & G Publishing, Manteo, NC (North Carolina)

A Taste of Virginia History ©2004 by Debbie Nunley, and Karen Jane Elliott, John F. Blair Publishers, Winston-Salem, NC (Virginia)

Tea-Time at the Masters ©1977 Junior League of Augusta, GA (Georgia)

Tennessee's 95 Magic Mixes: Second Helping ©1982 American Cancer Society Tennessee Division, Inc., Nashville, TN (Tennessee)

Tidewater on the Half Shell ©1985 Junior League of Norfolk-Virginia Beach, VA (Virginia)

Toast to Tidewater ©2004 Junior League of Norfolk-Virginia Beach, VA (Virginia)

Tony Chachere's Second Helping ©1995 Tony Chachere's Creole Foods of Opelousas, LA (Louisiana)

Treasured Family Favorites, by Alisa L. Pate, Cleveland, MS (Mississippi)

Treasures from Hope ©2003 Haven of Hope, Benton, KY (Kentucky)

Trim & Terrific American Favorites ©1996 Holly B. Clegg, Baton Rouge, LA (Louisiana)

Trim & Terrific One-Dish Favorites ©1997 Holly B. Clegg, Inc., Baton Rouge, LA (Louisiana)

Tropical Settings ©1995 The Junior League of Ft. Myers, FL (Florida)

Tropical Tastes, and Tantalizing Tales ©1993 by Carol Garvin, Coconut Grove, FL (Florida)

True Grits ©1995 Junior League of Atlanta, GA (Georgia)

Very Virginia ©1995 Junior League of Hampton Roads, Inc., Newport News, VA (Virginia)

Virginia Cook Book ©2001 Golden West Publications, Compiled by Janice Therese Mancusa, Phoenix, AZ (Virginia)

Virginia Seasons ©1984 The Junior League of Richmond, VA (Virginia)

Virginia Traditions ©1994 Junior Woman's Club of Hopewell, VA (Virginia)

When Dinnerbells Ring ©1978 Talladega Junior Welfare League, Talladega, AL (Alabama)

Windsor Academy Cookbook ©1988 Ponder's, Inc., by Windsor Academy, Thomasville, GA (Georgia)

Woman's Exchange Cookbook I ©1964, 1967 The Woman's Exchange of Memphis, TN (Tennessee)

Index

Key Lime Cake